Robert Burton

Twayne's English Authors Series

Arthur F. Kinney, Editor

University of Massachusetts, Amherst

TEAS 426

ROBERT BURTON
(1576–1640)
The Brasenose portrait, painted in 1635
Reproduced with the kind permission of the
Governing Body of Brasenose College, Oxford

Robert Burton

By Michael O'Connell

*University of California,
Santa Barbara*

Twayne Publishers • *Boston*

Robert Burton

Michael O'Connell

Copyright © 1986 by G.K. Hall & Co.
All Rights Reserved
Published by Twayne Publishers
A Division of G.K. Hall & Co.
70 Lincoln Street
Boston, Massachusetts 02111

Copyediting supervised by Lewis DeSimone
Book production by Elizabeth Todesco
Book design by Barbara Anderson

Typeset in 11 pt. Garamond
by Modern Graphics, Inc., Weymouth, Massachusetts

Printed on permanent/durable acid-free paper
and bound in the United States of America

Library of Congress Cataloging in Publication Data

O'Connell, Michael, 1943–
  Robert Burton.

  (Twayne's English authors series; TEAS 426)
  Bibliography: p. 117
  Includes index.
  1. Burton, Robert, 1577–1640—Criticism and
interpretation. I. Title. II. Series.
PR2224.036 1986   828'.309   86–365
ISBN 0-8057-6919-6

For Lisa
Remedium melius

Contents

About the Author

A native of Seattle, Washington, Michael O'Connell took his B.A. from the University of San Francisco in 1966 and his M. Phil. and Ph.D from Yale University (1969,1971). Since 1970 he has been a member of the English department of the University of California at Santa Barbara, where he teaches Renaissance literature. He is the author of *Mirror and Veil: the Historical Dimension of Spenser's Faerie Queene* (University of North Carolina Press, 1977), and of articles on Spenser, Elizabethan drama, Milton and Handel, Petrarch, and Catullus in various scholarly journals. He has also edited and translated the *Elisaeis* of William Alabaster, a fragmentary Neo-Latin epic on Queen Elizabeth, and has contributed a number of articles to the forthcoming *Spenser Encyclopedia*. Professor O'Connell has received a National Endowment for the Humanities fellowship and a research grant from the American Philosophical Society.

Editor's Note

Douglas Bush thought of Robert Burton as "sitting between Bacon and Hobbes, [where] he appears as a kind of gargoyle between the two spires of the cathedral of English scientific thought." Michael O'Connell's new and careful study of Burton's life and work substantially enlarges this claim. In providing the fullest biography of Burton now in print, O'Connell shows how books and libraries became both Burton's life and his chief metaphor and how his greatest work, the many accretive editions of the *Anatomy of Melancholy,* was a deliberate zigzagging which counterpoints scientific treatise (the first of the self-help books) with that of a fantasy of the exploring imagination and memory. To reinforce his paradox of a book, O'Connell argues, Burton forged his own macaronic prose, larding his English liberally with a Latin which he translates, elaborates, and puns on by turn. The largest part of this useful general study of Burton's canon is given over to an examination of the organization, sources, style, and themes of the *Anatomy,* but this book concludes as well with a detailed examination of some of the best of Burton's minor poems and his little-known play *Philosophaster.* For anyone who wishes to find ways to approach the *Anatomy* or to understand better the man and mind behind one of the unique masterpieces of all English literature, this will be a rewarding and constant companion.

—Arthur F. Kinney

Preface

Over fifty years have passed since Paul Jordan-Smith recommended Robert Burton's *Anatomy of Melancholy* as the perfect book for the hypothetical desert island whose library is confined to a single volume. In it, he suggested, is something for everyone. Nearly every field of human interest finds its way into Burton's book, all touched upon with wit and common sense. But readers, it must be admitted, have not rushed to buy up Burton's book against such an island sojourn, and no new edition has appeared in over half a century. Few undergraduate literature students make the acquaintance of its lively prose. And even among professional scholars of the seventeenth century, a surprisingly small number have more than sampled its curious wares. Burton's book is best known by its reputation—as an immense dissertation on abnormal psychology filled with the quaint learning of past ages and leavened with odd humor.

There is no mystery about the reasons for Burton's limited readership. The complexity that has deterred editors has had the same effect on readers. For one thing, Burton loves to quote in Latin and assumes his reader has a corresponding affection for reading it. His quotations come from over 1250 writers, from the entire range of European literature and science, most often identified but sometimes not. Frequently he translates his Latin quotations, but just as frequently he doesn't. Then there is the hefty bulk of the *Anatomy,* three volumes and some twelve hundred pages in the Everyman edition. And finally the subject matter: the black humor itself. Can there possibly be a readership for a huge, Latin-studded book on the depression that afflicted the Renaissance?

One who would write a book on Burton and his *Anatomy* obviously thinks so. To claim that it has something for everyone is to oversell it. But it has always been a book for the bookish, for those fascinated by the processes of learning. It is a book beloved of Dr. Johnson, of Sterne, Lamb, Byron, and Keats. In our own day it has drawn from Anthony Burgess the comment that "most modern books weary me, but Burton never does." (Burgess also took from Burton a hint for his own *Eve of St. Venus.*) The common thread of fascination with Burton is not so much his personality (although that is part of it) as his voracious appetite for books. He is not the charming, quaint old man as he has sometimes been portrayed. Though witty and sometimes whimsical, he can also be irascible and bitter, and as we learn in his book, he was a deeply discontented man. But he was intoxicated by books and libraries; they were clearly life to him. If melancholy is his explicit subject, books and the knowledge they make possible are his implicit, and finally more important, subject. The research library comprised mainly of printed books was a new technology in Burton's lifetime, and his preoccupation with it, which was also the preoccupation of his humanist contemporaries, is expressed on every page of the *Anatomy*. Our own preoccupation may be the technology of computers, but even their utility rests upon the power of the great libraries we take almost for granted. In Burton's lifetime centuries of thought suddenly became available in one place. A great part of the appeal of *The Anatomy of Melancholy*, I shall suggest, rests in the way it is caught up in the process of making negotiable this wealth of knowledge. Burton stands at the center of this process, attempting to master the power of a technology his culture has not yet assimilated.

There are some signs that the late twentieth century may see a revival of interest in Burton. Foremost among these is the new scholarly edition of the *Anatomy* which is promised for the end of this decade. It seems somehow fitting—and Burton would be keenly interested in the fact—that a proper edition of his book has had to wait upon a team of editors armed with the computer technology of our age. But the complexity of representing the growth of Burton's text through six editions and discovering the source and accuracy of his thousands of quotations has proved an insurmountable task for the single editor. A desired result of such an edition is that readers will no longer feel as mystified, or as intimidated, by the strangeness of Burton's scholarship. There may be comfort in knowing that the scholarly technology of our age has brought the *Anatomy* under some control. Another sign of renewed interest is the quality of the modest body of scholarship on Burton in the past twenty-odd years. Some of this has made a beginning in elucidating his relation to some of the Renaissance writers he cites. Other criticism has brought Burton into the circle of our own specific concerns with the nature of verbal discourse.

The present book is a "life and works" study designed to introduce Burton and the book that was his lifelong project. Because there is no standard biography available in English, I begin with a disproportionately long chapter on his life. In the more than twenty years since Jean Robert Simon's French study, quite a number of new biographical facts have come to light. The old commonplace that we know little about Burton the man is no longer true; in fact, the researches of a number of Burton scholars have told us more about his life than we know of most private men of the period. Still, there is much that we don't know, as Burton no doubt intended, and we must assume that a life given over to assiduous study and writing is not likely to leave behind an impressive trail of external detail. Readers who are interested rather in the *Anatomy* should turn to chapter 2, which is designed as an introduction to the book whose writing and augmentation absorbed Burton's life. Chapter 3 is a further study of the *Anatomy;* in it I have attempted a closer description of the book and the ways in which Burton transformed his subject. It cannot be claimed that every part of his book equally repays a reader's attention; there are arid stretches, especially in the medical parts, where even Burton's energy appears to wane. Since few of his sections, members, and subsections depend on what went before, a reader should not feel compelled to read the *Anatomy* consecutively. Though the primary purpose of chapter 3 is to develop an argument about the book, a new reader of Burton might find it useful as a guide. Burton's style has long been considered one of the reasons for reading him, and chapter 4 essays description and analysis; in it I attempt to account for a feature of his style that everyone notices but no one has commented on: its heavy reliance on Latin quotation. The final chapter concerns Burton's minor works, *Philosophaster,* his academic Latin comedy, and his Latin poems that appeared in various Oxford commemorative volumes.

Except when I am quoting an early edition, all citations of the *Anatomy of Melancholy* are to the Everyman edition, introduction by Holbrook Jackson, 3 vols. (London: J.M. Dent, 1932; reprint, 1964). To enable a reader to find the citation in another edition, I give in parentheses a reference first to the part, section, member, and subsection of the *Anatomy,* then the volume and page number of the Everyman edition. The Everyman edition provides a translation in brackets of the Latin which Burton does not translate; frequently, however, I have preferred to give my own translation.

In such cases I have silently substituted mine for the Everyman version in the brackets following the Latin.

I have been fortunate in the debts I have incurred in the writing of this book. The Research Committee of the Academic Senate of the University of California, Santa Barbara, has given support to my work. Bernard Richards, curator of pictures of Brasenose College, arranged to have the painting of Burton photographed and gave permission for its reproduction as the frontispiece. John Wing, assistant librarian of Christ Church, graciously opened the collection of Burton's books to me. Nicholas Kiessling generously made his own research on Burton's library available to me while I was working at Christ Church, shared his extensive knowledge of Burton with me when I was at an early stage of my work on the biography, and has since replied promptly to a number of questions. My colleague Richard Helgerson has listened to and helped refine some of my notions about Burton; he has also read the manuscript and made a number of helpful suggestions. My greatest debt I acknowledge in the dedication. My wife, Lisa, ever a votaress of the sanguine humor, has made contributions large and small to the progress of this book; among them has been to read every word and never fail of good stylistic advice.

Michael O'Connell

University of California, Santa Barbara

Chronology

1576 25 May, Robert Burton conceived, by his own reckoning, at 9 P.M.

1577 8 February, born at Lindley, in Leicestershire, at 8:44 A.M., under the sign of Saturn.

1593 Enters Brasenose College, Oxford.

1597 May have consulted Simon Forman, the astrological physician, during the summer and fall with physical complaints related to melancholy.

1599 Named a Student of Christ Church, Oxford, where he would live for the rest of his life.

1602 Graduates Bachelor of Arts, 30 June. Bodleian Library opens on 8 November.

1603 Contributes Latin poem to *Academiae Oxoniensis Pietas Erga Jacobum Regem* celebrating King James's accession.

1605 Graduates Master of Arts, 9 June; contributes to *Alba,* a play performed for King James's visit to Oxford in late August; his Latin poem celebrating the visit included in *Musa hospitalis, Ecclesiae Christi in adventum Jacobi Regis.*

1612 Contributes Latin poem on the death of Prince Henry to *Justa Oxoniensium.* Writes a Latin preface for second edition of Latin-English dictionary revised by his friend Francis Holyoke.

1613 Contributes Latin poem on the marriage of Princess Elizabeth and Frederick, the elector Palatine, to *Epithalamia, sive Lusus Palatini.* Contributes three Latin poems marking the death of Thomas Bodley to *Justa Funebria Ptolemmaei Oxoniensis Thomae Bodleii.*

1614 16 May, graduates Bachelor of Divinity.

1615 Named Clerk of the Market of Oxford on October 10; term renewed in two successive years.

1616 29 November, becomes vicar of St. Thomas the Martyr, Oxford.

1617   *Philosophaster* performed at Shrovetide festivities, 16 February. Contributes Latin poem on James's return from Scotland to *Jacobi Ara* and one for the third edition of the dictionary revised by Holyoke.

1619   Contributes Latin poem on the death of Queen Anne to *Academiae Oxoniensis, Funebria Sacra*.

1620   5 December, completes *Anatomy of Melancholy*.

1621   *Anatomy of Melancholy* published in quarto by Henry Cripps of Oxford.

1622   Contributes Latin poem on the death of Sir Henry Savile to *Ultima Linea Savilii*.

1623   Contributes Latin poem on Prince Charles's return from Spain to *Carolus Redux*.

1624   Second edition of the *Anatomy*, in folio. Receives living of Walesby in Lincolnshire from Dowager Countess of Exeter; receives advowson (legal reversion) of living of Seagrave in Leicestershire from George, Lord Berkeley. Contributes Latin poem on death of William Camden to *Camdeni Insignia*.

1625   Contributes Latin poem on death of King James to *Oxoniensis Academiae Parentalia;* marks marriage of King Charles and Henrietta Maria with Latin poem in *Epithalamia Oxoniensia*.

1626   Named librarian of Christ Church library.

1628   Third edition of the *Anatomy*, in folio.

1630   Contributes Latin poem on birth of Prince Charles to *Britanniae Natalis*.

1632   25 June, becomes rector of Seagrave (resigns living of Walesby before 1632). Fourth edition of the *Anatomy*, in folio.

1633   Contributes Latin poem on Charles I's return from Scotland to *Solis Britannici Perigaeum*. Marks birth of Prince James with Latin poem in *Vitis Carolinae Gemma Altera*.

1636   Contributes Latin poems on birth of Princess Elizabeth to *Flos Britannicus Veris Novissimi* and to *Coronae Carolinae Quadratura*.

1638   Fifth edition of the *Anatomy*, in folio. Contributes Latin and English verses on death of Lord Bayning to *Death Repealed*.

1639   15 August, draws up his last will and testament.

1640   Dies 25 January; buried two days later in Christ Church Cathedral.

1651   Sixth edition of *Anatomy* published, corrected and "with severall considerable Additions" made by Burton before his death.

Chapter One
The Man and the Book

More than that of any other writer of his age, Robert Burton's life was defined and expressed by the printed book. From the time he went up to Oxford at the age of sixteen until his death forty-seven years later, books held his constant attention. He lived his life in libraries, in that of his own college, Christ Church, which he served as librarian, in the new university library opened by Thomas Bodley in 1602, and amid his own formidable collection of books. His reading was immense, and it found expression in the book whose composition and revision occupied his entire life. Seldom in fact have a life and book been so closely identified as Burton's and his *Anatomy of Melancholy*. The greater part of what we know of him is found in references scattered through the pages of his immense work. After the first edition was published in 1621, he continually tinkered with the book, revising in part, but mostly adding to it. After bringing out new editions in 1624 and 1628, he vowed in the preface to the latter not to return to the work again: *"Ne quid nimis.* I will not hereafter add, alter, or retract; I have done."* But he hadn't reckoned on how much his life was bound up with the growth of his book. Another revised edition appeared four years later, then a fifth in 1638. Shortly before his death in 1640 he handed an annotated copy of this edition over to his publisher, and from it a sixth edition was printed in 1651. Whatever he may have meant by it, the epitaph Burton composed for his tomb in Christ Church Cathedral suggests something of the obsessive tie between the book and the life. Calling himself not by his own name but by the name of his persona in the book, Democritus Junior, he asserts that he is one to whom Melancholy gave life and death, "cui vitam dedit et mortem Melancholia." Melancholy is of course the morbid state of mind from which Burton, and much of the age, claimed to suffer. But it was also the object of his life's researches and the title of the book that gave them expression.

So bookish a life has not tempted literary biographers.[1] A man who lived his life in libraries, who never traveled, married, held

1

office, or left behind him a record of involvement in any of the
controversies of a contentious age, may scarcely appear to have lived
at all. Nor is Burton a Montaigne or a Thomas Browne, who in
their quietude achieved a rich and varied inner life. When he reflects,
he does so in a way that expresses a personality not so much isolated
and individual as continuous with the books surrounding him. He
can frequently be witty and amusing, and in his style we hear the
genuine sound of a voice speaking. Both the wit and the voice come
of a mind that has just been directed to the book open before it.
No human mind or personality can be said to be wholly transparent,
perfectly expressive of a tradition or an age. And yet more than
anyone else Burton expresses the culmination of a tradition of scholarship, the desire to know and be known through books, that began
a century and a half before in the early Renaissance. Through him
that tradition spoke more volubly than it did in any of his
contemporaries.

Childhood at Lindley and Grammar School

Burton tells us in the *Anatomy* that he "was born of worshipful
parents . . . in an ancient family, but I am a younger brother"
(2.3.2;2:142). He also gives his nativity: "Saturn was the lord of
my geniture, culminating, etc., and Mars principal significator of
manners, in partile conjunction with mine ascendant; both fortunate
in their houses, etc." (Democritus Junior to the Reader; 1:18). We
might consider it a measure of our distance from Burton that we
would find the simple date more revealing, but probably we owe
our own interest in birth dates, and indeed the recording of the
exact time of birth, to the sixteenth-century practice of casting
nativities. In notes that Burton made in his astrological books we
learn not only the day and hour of his birth, 8:44 A.M. on 8 February
1577, but also the precise time of his conception. He believed he
was conceived at 9 o'clock in the evening of 25 May 1576.[2] Was
such information, we wonder, communicated between sixteenth-
century parents and children? A mere educated guess, based on
knowledge of his birth date and his parents' bedtime, would have
no useful status in astrological calculation.

Burton could not take great comfort from his nativity, and even
the detail that both influences were "fortunate in their houses" did
not dispel the clouds that hung over a Saturnian like himself.[3] For

the "lord of the geniture" was believed to be the decisive influence since this gave the body its constitution and temperament. If Saturn was dominant in one's nativity and caused melancholy in the temperament, then, Burton recognized, "he shall be very austere, sullen, churlish, black of colour, profound in his cogitations, full of cares, miseries, and discontents, sad and fearful, always silent, solitary, still delighting in husbandry, in woods, orchards, gardens, rivers, ponds, pools, dark walks and close" (1.3.1.3;1:397–98). But the influence of Mars, if strong and fortunate, can be seen as offsetting or tempering to some extent the Saturnian influence. For Mars would make a man bold and outgoing, spirited, a witty conversationalist, eager to rule and perhaps rash and quick to take offense. Mars would also impart an energy for work, a restless interest in a variety of projects. Though Burton knew himself doomed to the temperament of a Saturnian, he must have taken some comfort in seeing the possibilities offered in exploiting his Martian side. All of the signs in his nativity pointed to a wretched love-life, one which seemed to exclude marriage and to be fraught with dangers of perversion and unrestrained lust.[4] Taken as a whole, it was not a happy prognostic, all the more so in that Burton developed an enduring fascination with astrology which tended to assure some of its fulfillment.

Burton was the fourth child, and second son, of Ralph and Dorothy Burton, who were married on 2 October 1571, some five and a half years before Robert's birth. At the time of his marriage Ralph Burton was the twenty-four-year-old squire of Lindley, in Leicestershire. His twenty-one-year-old bride, Dorothy Faunt, came from Foston, a village some twenty miles away. We learn of the composition of the Burton family from a record that Ralph Burton kept in the opening pages of a small medieval manuscript, as a later age would do with a family Bible.[5] The content of the manuscript, a canon of statutes of English law in Latin and Anglo-Norman from the early fourteenth century, does not seem particularly relevant to the use to which Ralph Burton put it, but perhaps its antiquity, as great as the walls of Lindley Hall itself, commended it to this solemn use. There he registered first the birth of Elizabeth, named no doubt in honor of the queen, on 7 July 1573. Another daughter, Anne, followed a year later, on 5 July. Then the first son and heir was born 24 August 1575, and christened William, perhaps after the Burton ancestor who is named in the precious manuscript as its original owner and the bearer of the royal standard. William, a

future topographer of Leicestershire, would continue the tradition
of recording births in the family manuscript; later he would also
supplement his father's record by supplying the dates of death of
his father, grandfather, and other ancestors for two generations back.
It was an age of intense concern for history, familial as well as
national. Robert was born eighteen months later, followed by five
more children: Mary, George, Jane, Ralph, and Catherine.[6] Five
years after Catherine's birth, Ralph Burton noted the birth of a final
child, a daughter Dorothy, who died as an infant. Later Robert
would record the nativities of each of his living siblings in the same
copy of Stadius's *Ephemerides* where he noted his own (and William's)
conception and birth. Did the nativities indicate to him that all of
his sisters but Catherine would die in their thirties?[7] Such were the
perils of seventeenth-century childbearing. But in his own family
nine children surviving infancy—and the mother surviving ten
births—must be considered an exceptionally successful example of
sixteenth-century breeding.

Lindley Hall, the family manor, appears in a stylized engraving
on the title page of William Burton's *Description of Leicestershire*
(1622).[8] The engraving shows a square moat surrounding an island
with a wooded park on three sides and a formal garden on the
fourth. The building is clearly medieval, perhaps two centuries old
by the late sixteenth century. On the garden side rises a rather stark
façade broken only by two sets of round towers on either side topped
with pointed, cone-shaped roofs. This building doubtless contained
the hall and dining chambers of the estate. Behind this two narrow
buildings and a third at right angles formed a square enclosing a
large yard. At one of the towers of the façade a footbridge spanned
the moat, and on the far side a range of buildings, probably stables,
protected the bridge, like the barbican of a castle, from access. This
in itself betrays the comparative antiquity of Lindley Hall, for by
the late sixteenth century there was no longer a need for aristocrats
or gentry to build defensible manorhouses. By then large windows
and attractive façades had replaced defensive moats and barbicans.
William Burton tells us that the manor had come to the family
early in the sixteenth century when his great-grandfather had married Elizabeth Hardwick, whose inheritance it was. Much of the
manor must have been forested, for William calls it "a kind of
wood-land soile, and apt for wood," though also good for pasture
and grain.[9] One of its peculiarities, he adds, is that snakes, adders,

and lizards are never seen in the estate, though common enough in the surrounding countryside. The Lindley Hall that the Burton family knew would not survive the seventeenth century; it was torn down to make way for a building more in keeping with the classical taste of the late century, which in turn has also fallen into ruin.[10] The great love of the country that Burton professes in the *Anatomy* (2.2.4;2:79)—also a characteristic of the Saturnian man—must be bound up with his childhood in rural Leicestershire.

It is from his mother that Burton inherited the interest in medicine that informs so much of the *Anatomy*. There he testifies to her "excellent skill in chirurgery, sore eyes, aches, etc., and such experimental medicines, as all the country where she dwelt can witness, to have done many famous and good cures upon divers poor folks, that were otherwise destitute of help" (2.5.1.6;2:250). "Chirurgery" here does not have quite our modern sense of surgery, of opening the body to remove or repair diseased organs, though it does overlap with it to a degree. The word had still its etymological sense of medicine practiced with the hands and would include such things as bone-setting and the treatment of sprains and lacerations. The context of Burton's recollection of his mother's skill and charity is revealing also of the sort of medicine practiced by a woman of Dorothy Burton's place as lady of the manor. He is in fact telling a story on himself, how on a vacation to visit his parents at Lindley, by this time no doubt possessed of some academic knowledge of medicine, he scoffed at her treatment of an ague by an amulet of a spider in a nutshell. What has a spider to do with a fever, he asked himself. Then later, "rambling amongst authors (as I often do)," he came upon this very remedy "in Dioscorides, approved by Matthiolus, repeated by Aldrovandus" (2.5.1.5;2:250). There must, then, be something to it. Clearly no hard-and-fast distinction can be made between the medicine practiced by a gentlewoman presiding over a country neighborhood and the medicine an unlettered wise woman might practice. And Burton's discovery of his mother's treatment in his books suggests that academic medicine had not finished learning from folk medicine in the seventeenth century. Given the nature of prescientific medicine, one may hesitate to credit too much of the family's good health—and the survival of nine of the ten Burton children—to these maternal skills, but it is not impossible that some of the "famous and good cures" her son credits her with may have been performed on her own family.

From his mother's milk Burton may have sucked more than his
fascination with medicine. Melancholy seems also to have run in
the maternal line. In his *Description of Leicestershire* brother William
records that their mother's brother Anthony Faunt, who had been
designated lieutenant general of the country's forces against the
Armada in 1588, died of melancholy after the Earl of Huntington
denied him the post. Another maternal uncle became a Jesuit.
William tells how Arthur Faunt left Oxford at the age of fourteen
with his tutor and entered the Jesuit college in Louvain in 1568.[11]
This must have been a family scandal at the time, but both William
and Robert would later record the connection with some pride.
William lists eleven books by his uncle and concludes by saying
that he was "a man of great learning, gravity and wisdome, and for
his religious life held in great esteem." Robert makes the note in
a copy he owned of one of this uncle's books that he was rector of
the Jesuit college at Posnan in Poland and died in Lithuania in
1595.[12] Though he never knew this uncle, he appears to have valued
this connection to a relative who had also led an academic life and
taken part, even if on the wrong side, in the theological debates of
the century. Though never a friend to the Jesuits, Burton seems in
this case to have allowed family feeling to take precedence over
religious ideology.

In a discussion of salubrious air in the *Anatomy* Burton mentions
that he attended grammar school at Sutton Coldfield in Warwick-
shire (2.2.3;2:63). But in his will he also refers to Nuneaton, some
three miles from Lindley Hall, "where I was once a Grammar Scholar."
No doubt he attended both, perhaps beginning closer to home at
Nuneaton, then proceeding on to Sutton Coldfield. Burton leaves
some reflections in the *Anatomy* that suggest bitterness about this
early schooling. He lists education second among the accidental
causes of melancholy, and writes of "tyrannical, impatient, hair-
brain schoolmasters" who are as bad in their way "as hangmen and
executioners":

They make many children endure a martyrdom all the while they are at
school; with a bad diet, if they board in their houses, too much severity
and ill-usage, they quite pervert their temperature of body and mind: still
chiding, railing, frowning, lashing, tasking, keeping, that they are *fracti
animis*, moped many times, weary of their lives, *nimia severitate deficiunt
et desperant* [through harsh treatment they become dull and dispirited],

and think no slavery in the world (as I once did myself) like to that of a grammar scholar. (1,2,4,2;1:333)

Such complaints are frequent in the period, and whether or not they were a leading cause of melancholy, harsh schoolmasters must have occasioned as much misery as correct Latinity among sixteenth-century boys. Roger Ascham, whose book *The Scholemaster* appeared some fifteen years before the seven- or eight-year-old Burton began his schooling, was of the opinion that "over many" such masters were to be found all over England, indeed that it was "common use" for teaching and beating to go together.[13] Ascham felt that such practice was particularly harmful for the kind of student he valued most, the "hard wit," who required encouragement but repaid such attention with more solidity and retentiveness than the mercurial "quick wit." Burton, one imagines, was rather among the latter class of students, but he came to agree with Ascham's judgment that the effect on a student of an ill-tempered schoolmaster was rather to "break him than bow him, rather mar him than mend him."

"Student of the Most Flourishing College of Europe"

It may have been with some relief, then, that Burton followed his older brother to Brasenose College, Oxford, in 1593. Brasenose had been founded in 1512 by William Smyth, bishop of Lincoln, at a time when humanist learning and culture was first making its influence felt in England. But unlike the two other Oxford colleges founded in this decade, Corpus Christi and Cardinal College (later Christ Church after the fall of its founder, Cardinal Wolsey), Brasenose had been conservatively directed toward the scholastic learning of medieval Oxford.[14] At the time of Burton's matriculation it was a college to which country squires sent their sons. As at the other Oxford colleges, the education was still designed to form a clergyman in the Church of England, though this was changing in the second half of the sixteenth century.[15] Discipline at Brasenose appears to have been relatively strict. Corporal punishment was not unknown, and fines were meted out for such infractions as speaking English, using abusive language, fighting, and violations of the parietal rules. Undergraduates, of course, were under the direct supervision of a tutor, whose role was as much in loco parentis as educational. Anthony à Wood says Burton "made considerable progress in logic and philosophy."[16] But if Brasenose left any impression on him, it was insufficiently strong to find any expression in the *Anatomy*; the six years he was enrolled there remain a blank. In 1599, while still an undergraduate, he was named a Student of Christ Church, equivalent to a Fellow in the other Oxford colleges. His pride in this affiliation stands in suggestive contrast to his silence about Brasenose. In the early pages of the *Anatomy* he declares that he has "been brought up a student in the most flourishing college of Europe, *augustissimo collegio,*" and having enjoyed the use of libraries as good as those of the Vatican, he would be loath to be found so unprofitable a scholar of "so learned and noble a society" as that of Christ Church (Democritus Junior to the Reader; 1:17).

The silence about Brasenose may not, however, be taken as an unequivocal judgment of the college. An oddity of Burton's undergraduate years is their length. He did not receive his bachelor's degree until June 1602, at age twenty-five, nine years after he came to the university, rather than the usual three or four. It seems plausible that Burton, like another Oxford undergraduate, Samuel Johnson, a century later, suffered a prolonged bout of melancholy, or an illness that occasioned melancholy, during this period of his life. He tells us in the *Anatomy* that he "was not a little offended by this malady," and that he writes of melancholy "by being busy to avoid melancholy" (Democritus Junior to the Reader; 1:20–21). If he was troubled by illness or melancholy, it is likely that he spent a substantial part of those six years not at Brasenose but at Lindley Hall.

This conjecture that illness may have seriously interrupted his schooling is supported by evidence that a Robert Burton, aged twenty, consulted Simon Forman, the astrological physician, in London five times in the summer and fall of 1597.[17] Could this be the same Robert Burton? He too was twenty years old in 1597, and the consultations could have taken place while he was staying with his brother William, who was living at the Inner Temple at the time. If only Forman had left a record of his patient's nativity, this would have settled the matter. But the coincidence of the name and age and our subject's intense interest in the illness for which Forman treated his patient make the conjecture plausible. The young man who came to Forman in the late afternoon of 18 June 1597 represented a dangerous case, Forman recorded, "a great heaviness & drowsiness in the hed . . . moch wind in the bowells." Noting pain in the head and stomach and a sluggishness in the blood, Forman diagnosed melancholy and considered it likely that the young man would contract palsy or a quartan fever. Most dire was the doctor's conclusion: "he carieth death upon him . . . and will die suddenly." Forman recommended three days of preparation, then a purge. A week later the patient returned, still suffering distress in his head, nose, and stomach. Forman gave him some pills this time. Not quite a month later, on 21 July, the young man came back to Forman with much the same complaints he had earlier had. Forman was again concerned about a "melancholy reum [rheum] roning to the reins and belly and stopping the vains which will cause a fever & vexaton of the mind some 17 dais hence." Again he gave him a purge. If it worked, the relief was only temporary, for at their next consultation on 19 August, the complaints were much the same. At their final consultation on 11 October, the patient was still troubled by "a wind in the belly," but the other complaints had modulated to "a burning in his hands and knees." After this the twenty-year-old Robert Burton either experienced a remission of his complaints or found another physician, for he did not return to Forman.

Two years later, in 1599, we find Burton resuming his studies, now at Christ Church. "For form's sake, tho' he wanted not a tutor," Wood says, "he was put under the tuition of Dr. John Bancroft."[18] Burton could hardly have asked for a better-connected tutor. Nephew of the bishop of London and future archbishop of Canterbury, Bancroft had been educated at Westminster School and elected a student of Christ Church in 1592. Though only three years older than Burton, Bancroft was some six or seven years ahead of him in his studies; he had just taken his M.A. degree and two years later would leave Oxford for a series of livings to which his uncle would prefer him. In 1610 he would return to Oxford as a master of University College, where he devoted himself to improving the college's financial position. Bancroft was a high churchman, later a friend of Archbishop Laud and an enemy to the Puritans. It seems likely that some degree of friendship developed between the tutor and his bookish scholar. In the *Anatomy* Burton refers approvingly of Cuddesdon, the palace some five miles distant from Oxford that Bancroft began building for the see of Oxford shortly after he was named bishop in 1632. His praise of its pleasant site, "in a good air, good prospect, good soil, both for profit and pleasure," and his comment that it "is lately and fairly built" suggest that he was a frequent guest of his old tutor after the palace was completed in 1635 (2.2.3;2:64).[19]

Burton was awarded the degrees of Bachelor of Arts on 30 June 1602 and Master of Arts on 9 June 1605. In addition he had to pass through various college ranks as well: the *discipulus* of 1599 became *philosophus secundi vicenarii* in December 1603, then *philosophus primi vicenarii* in December 1607.[20] Having attained this last rank, Burton would then have been assigned as a tutor to beginning scholars. The role of tutor was central in seventeenth-century Oxford. His duties were not only educational, advising his students what to study, how to study, and what books they should read, but social and moral as well. He assumed responsibility for supervising their finances (sometimes paying out an allowance from money received from parents) and acting as a guide to proper conversation, manners, dress, and conduct toward superiors and inferiors.[21] It was the tutor's duty to see that his scholars formed proper religious opinions and practices. A good tutor made all the difference. He not only guided his students through the curriculum in logic, rhetoric, history, and philosophy, but also made recommendations as to what other books, even those in English, they should read. Burton's own wide reading would therefore have made him an invaluable resource to his scholars. But we cannot otherwise judge his effectiveness as a tutor. Given his duties, education is a curious absence from the subjects discussed in the *Anatomy*.

Such relationships could be as significant and fruitful for the tutor as for the scholar. It has been suggested that Burton acted as tutor to Robert Smith, son of the dowager countess of Exeter, from whom he received the living of Walesby in 1624.[22] Less certain is his relationship with George Lord Berkeley, to whom he dedicated the *Anatomy* in 1621 and from whom he received his principal piece of patronage, the living of Seagrave in Leicestershire. But Burton's acquaintance with him must date from around the time of Berkeley's entrance into Christ Church as an eighteen-year-old undergraduate in 1619. The feeling references to patronage and ambition scattered throughout the *Anatomy* suggest that Burton was far from indifferent to what his students might later do for him. But these are the only two from whom he received any valuable return. The deaneries and bishoprics went to better-connected, or more effectively ambitious, men.

From the time of the award of his bachelor's degree, Burton assumed his place as one of the permanent members of the society of Christ Church. At the accession of King James in 1603 he contributed ten lines of Latin verse to the volume with which Oxford honored the event. Two years later he made a similar offering to the volume of verses celebrating James's first royal visit to Oxford.[23] On this latter occasion he based the conceit for his poem on the position of the stars on the day of the royal arrival: the Sun, joined with Venus and Mercury, was in the house of Virgo. James must be the Sun, his queen Venus, and Prince Henry Mercury; the house of Virgo, then, is Christ Church, where James and his court lodged during the visit. So often therefore as this conjunction of stars comes around, so often will these gods bestow their presence upon the scholars, and so often great James may visit again his Christ Church. The amusing extravagance of the conceit owes more to silver-age Roman example than to contemporary metaphysical verse.

Burton also took an active part in the entertainment the college prepared for the king and court. Some two weeks before the royal visit Burton wrote to his brother William, "heare is no newes but praeparation for the kinges coming, who will be heare on Tuesday come forth night." Among the plays and verses being readied for the visit, "that parte of ye play w^h I made is very well liked, especially those scenes of the Magus, and I have had greate thanks for my paynes of .D. Kinge o^r newe Deane."[24] The play, which does not survive, is assumed to be *Alba,* a pastoral probably in Latin but just possibly in English. Its subject was mythological and from its costume and property list appears to have included no less than Neptune, Apollo, Pan, Nestor, eight or ten kings, twenty nymphs, four hermits, ten satyrs, three "sylvanes," six morris dancers, and an old woman in addition to Burton's magician. The king arrived on Tuesday, 27 August 1605. Hopes at Christ Church must have been high that the king would approve, perhaps even enjoy, the elaborate spectacle prepared for him. Alas, the play was a disaster. The queen and her ladies were offended by "five or six men almost naked"—the satyrs or "sylvanes"?—and the king, according to the same witness, would have left before it was half over if the chancellors of both Oxford and Cambridge had not begged him to stay.[25] Even a theatrical flop deserves royal attention if it is tendered by loyal

subjects—and the most powerful college of the university. Our
sympathies may grow mixed, however, when we learn that the play
started between nine and ten o'clock at night, included a great many
country songs and dances, and wasn't over until one in the morning.
Burton and his collaborators had to content themselves with Dr.
King's good opinion.

And so apparently Burton did, for undeterred by the royal re-
ception he was back at work on another play the following year.
This was not a collaborative venture but entirely his own. And far
from the mythological (and choreographic) excesses of *Alba,* the new
play, also in Latin, stayed in a world of cozening and cozened
mortals. In fact, *Philosophaster* (or *The False Philosopher*) stayed within
a university, though the university is moved from between the
Thames and the Cherwell to Osuna in Spain.[26] In this way Burton
could indulge an academic taste for self-satire without fear of touch-
ing things too close to home, rather the way a contemporary academic novel can amuse itself with jargon and pretensions without
libeling the author's colleagues. *Philosophaster* must have been a
success with its first (and only) audience when it was finally staged
in the hall of Christ Church eleven years later, during the Shrovetide
festivities of 1617. It was acted, as was customary, by the students
themselves, the more demanding roles going to the older, more
experienced members and the women's and smaller parts to the
younger scholars. Three townsmen were enlisted to play the townsmen. In view of Dr. King's approval of Burton's first dramatic
efforts, there is some interest in his son's leading the cast list as the
duke of Osuna. Burton did not himself take a part, but he must
have had a hand, one supposes, in the direction. *Philosophaster* sports
amusingly with its audience's sense of shared experience. Burton
might even be accused of playing to his gallery when a couple of
courtesans decide the question of whether townsmen or scholars are
the best lovers resolutely in favor of the scholars. In spirit the satire
is directed outward at various academic charlatans, and it seems
unlikely that anyone in Burton's audience would have felt himself
touched too closely. But there is some bitterness directed toward
the pseudolearned academic operators who are able to "fish out fat
Benefices," while the genuine theologians, "pale from much study,"
are left to their Aquinas and Scotus. And the quack physician is
identified unequivocally as a Paracelsian. Polumathes, one of the
two genuine scholars, has indeed been to Oxford, where he was

disappointed to find that the only wise and learned men were the dead ones chained to the desks of the admirable library. Beyond the walls of the library, however, the arts and philosophy are in exile, and only law has any prestige. The complaint is a familiar one, of course, and *nominibus mutatis* we hear of the neglect of the humanities in favor of the business and engineering faculties. Such jokes as there are—Burton's epilogue rightly concedes their scarcity—have a comforting familiarity to them. Philosophers agree about as often as clocks. When one townsman complains that the scholars of the new university will make fun of them, his fellow with a better eye for the main chance replies, "Let them call me what they want, as long as they call me rich" (*Philosophaster*, 44–45). All ends happily in the overthrow of the charlatans and the reestablishment of the university through Polumathes and Philobiblos, with whose real learning the Christ Church audience was presumably able to identify. A song rhyming the triumph of philosophy, "to the tune of Bonny Nell," brought the occasion to a celebratory close.

Burton's Oxford

Though not a portrait of his Oxford, Burton's play does give us a sense that university and town were anything but dull. The posturing and competition among the false philosophers, the sexual energies of the students, the general merriment and drinking in the play point to a way of life not entirely dominated by academic routine. Much the same sense of Oxford emerges in the university and college statutes, which seem never to have been sufficient unto the day. New regulations were frequently in need to suppress the abundance of unlicensed alehouses, to keep the students from wearing gaudy or fashionable clothes, boots, or even spurs with their gowns, to make them cut their long hair and lovelocks, to suppress their carrying of weapons.[27] The regulations in particular indicate a society that was frequently rowdy, occasionally brawling, at times violent. Even the senior members of the university were quick to take, and give, offense; open insults among vice-chancellors, proctors, and masters were far from unknown. Among the colleges, which were self-governing and independent institutions, feuds could break out among the leadership as well as among the undergraduates.

In this regard it is worth noting that Burton's Oxford was very much a society of young men, younger on the whole than any modern university. The youngest students were around twelve, though most students came up to university at fifteen or sixteen. Since a successful academic career led most frequently to a beneficed living and departure from the university, the oldest members were seldom much past forty. Even the deans of Christ Church during Burton's time were typically in their late thirties or early forties when they assumed office, and since all but William Goodwin, who died in office in 1620, went on to a bishopric or cathedral deanery within ten years, even the leadership remained comparatively young.[28] Richard Corbet, who became dean in 1620 at the age of thirty-seven, may not be typical of the leaders of Christ Church, but he does show a style that was appreciated. A wit, a boon companion to Ben Jonson, and a player of pranks, Corbet was said to have "loved to the last boyes play very well."[29] One wonders if Burton was among the friends Corbet was with at a tavern in Abingdon one day when he heard a ballad singer complain about poor sales. Corbet, future bishop of Oxford and Norwich, threw off his gown, commandeered the ballad singer's leather jacket and began to sing ballads. Having a good voice and handsome person, he soon gathered a sizable audience and did a brisk business in ballads.

But Oxford of the early seventeenth century had another sort of liveliness more immediately relevant to Burton's purpose. On 8 November 1602 Thomas Bodley reopened the library of Duke Humphrey, whose restoration he had overseen—and paid for—during the previous four years. Oxford's libraries had fared badly in the Reformation years; much had been destroyed, and the whole university library, including Duke Humphrey's collection, was dispersed.[30] It is hardly accidental that Burton's great library of a book was conceived, gestated, and brought to birth during the very years that Bodley was doing the same for the offspring that would bear his name. By the end of 1602 the Bodleian Library contained two thousand volumes. In 1605 when the first printed catalog was issued, Bodley had so spectacularly succeeded in making donations the fashion that six thousand volumes were listed. The library's fame was such that nobles, churchmen, lawyers, and merchants vied to enrich it. From the beginning Bodley was, however, very particular about what books should be admitted; no playbooks, almanacs, popular books of marvels or jests were allowed in. (This created a gap that the bequest of Burton's library was later to remedy.) In 1610 an addition was needed, and the Arts End over the Proscholium was begun. The second catalog, printed in 1620, contained over sixteen thousand volumes. Burton's boast in the *Anatomy* that he had enjoyed a library as good as the Vatican that Paulus Jovius had used (Democritus Junior to the Reader; 1:17) was very nearly true.

This was also the time when Christ Church's own library came into being. Donations of books for a college library were made as early as 1581, but it was not until 1599, the year Burton entered, that a librarian was appointed.[31] He was at first simply a member who had taken his B.A. who then relinquished his post to another B.A. when he achieved the M.A. The library occupied the old refectory of St. Frideswide, on the site of which Christ Church had been founded by Wolsey seventy-five years before. Burton must have enjoyed its position just outside the center of the college and overlooking the quiet Christ Church meadows. In 1613 a certain Otho Nicholson gave eight hundred pounds to restore the building and another one hundred pounds for books. From this time on the library became a central concern of the college. The following year the librarian's position was upgraded (and the salary tripled to 10 shillings a term), and every graduate, B.A., M.A. or B.D., was required to contribute 13 shillings 4 pence, or a book of at least that value. (A new canon was assessed two pounds and a new dean five.) Often several graduates combined their resources to purchase a folio for the library. Burton received his bachelor of divinity degree in that year and was duly listed among the donors to the library.

In 1626 Burton was named librarian of Christ Church, which must have seemed an apt post for the member who most haunted the libraries of Oxford.[32] His duties can scarcely have been onerous. There were few regulations to enforce, and doubtless the daily tasks of opening and closing the library could be accomplished by deputy—or maybe it gave him an excuse, if he needed one, to arrive early and stay late. Readers were mainly left on their honor to respect the college's books, an honor bound by an impressive, mouth-filling Latin oath not "to steal, pawn, erase, deform, cut, annotate, write in, spoil, blot, contaminate or in any other way injure" the books.[33] One imagines that Burton, once he had cataloged the new acquisitions, found sufficient time for reading them.

Burton's Library

A third library that Burton haunted was his own, a substantial collection that at his death numbered over fifteen hundred titles.[34] Such a library was more than ten times the size of the usual library

kept by an Oxford don of the time. He was careful to identify his
ownership of his books. On the title page of most of them he signed
his name or initials, and after about 1599 he added as well a curious
cypher, three *r*s arranged in an inverted triangle. The cypher alludes
to his family arms, three dogs' heads similarly arranged in an inverted triangle on a blue shield; *r* was defined as the *littera canina*,
the "dog letter," because its sound approximated a dog's growl. In
addition Burton frequently listed the price he paid for the book and
the year he acquired it. These marks of ownership, as well as the
list compiled after his death, have enabled the identification of his
books in the Bodleian and the reassembling of the part of his library
that went to Christ Church. So it is possible to browse amid Burton's
books, even literally in the case of Christ Church, and to search for
glimpses of his habits of mind that supplement what we know from
the *Anatomy*.

His books confirm two things that we already know from the
Anatomy. First of all, they tell us that Burton lived his intellectual
life primarily in Latin. Though a large—and indeed surprising—
number of English titles are to be found, the majority of his books
are in Latin. The small handful of titles in Italian (three), Spanish,
German, and Hebrew (one each) suggests that he did not read those
languages easily or with pleasure. But more noteworthy for a scholar
of Burton's humanist culture is the lack of Greek books. Not even
a Greek New Testament is to be found. It is just possible, of course,
that he owned some Greek books and that these may have been the
ones his particular friends were allowed to select from his library
after his death. But he seldom quotes Greek in the *Anatomy* and
clearly preferred to read Greek authors in Latin translation.

The library also confirms that Burton's appetite for books was
not only voracious but omnivorous. No limits confined his reading.
His books convey the impression of a man who was a compulsive
reader and hoarder of the printed word. What may be surprising is
the currency of Burton's library. Kiessling notes that a large majority
of his books, 74 percent of them, were published in his own lifetime.
The impression of Burton as an antiquarian in his literary interests
is simply wrong. He continued to acquire the latest books in the
areas that particularly interested him. Books of theology and religious controversy are the largest single category of his library, 24
percent of the total, scarcely surprising given Burton's profession.
But the 20 percent devoted to literature, the 16 percent to history,

nine percent to medicine, six percent to government, five percent to geography and travel set him apart from most of his academic colleagues. And how many other Oxford dons, one wonders, owned jest books in English, cony-catching pamphlets, quartos of popular plays (though none of Shakespeare's), contemporary satires, pamphlets describing oddities and marvels, fantastic and speculative books, like John Wilkins's *Discovery of a world in the moone,* which Burton acquired a year before his death? This last class of books was just the sort of rubbish that Thomas Bodley had excluded from the university library. If Burton was to read it anywhere, he had to buy it himself. He must have frequently started reading a pamphlet in a bookstall, then become captivated enough to buy it and take it away with him. He clearly enjoyed hearing of oddities, marvels, and natural prodigies. His library points to a weakness for popular works that retailed the equivalent of today's sensational magazines, pamphlets with titles like *Gods worke in wonders, Miraculously shewen upon two women, lately delivered of two monsters, with a most strange and terrible earthquake, by which, fields and other grounds, were quite removed to other places* (1617). In part such things must have fed his sense of the strangeness and unpredictability of the world, his belief that there was more in heaven and earth than were dreamt of in his or anyone else's philosophy.

But another part of Burton's library suggests he may have been trying to make sense of just such events, wondering if they were indeed unpredictable. Works of astrology are a category not only well represented but particularly well used; as a group they are probably his most heavily annotated books. I have already noted the record he kept of his own and his siblings' nativities in his copy of Stadius's *Ephemerides;* there he also recorded an earthquake "magnus et admirabilis" that occurred on 6 April 1580, when he was three years old. Initials beside other dates indicated his interest in the nativities of others of his acquaintance. His copy of Ptolemy's *Quadripartum Opus* (in a Paris edition of 1519) was bound up with a volume that contained two sixteenth-century works, one by John Dee, the English astrologer and magus, and the other by Cyprianus Leovitius (Leowitz). Burton also had some forty blank pages bound into the book, and on these he made notes of his own on matters astronomical and astrological. Some of these are practical calculations needed for casting nativities, others notes on various astrological textbooks designed to supplement the printed works. As a whole, the volume comprised a kind of astrological handbook for Burton, a place where he had assembled what he needed for doing various astronomical operations.[35] Anthony à Wood says that he was "an exact mathematician" and "a curious calculator of nativities," and here we catch him at work. On the first page of the volume is a diagram of his own nativity, which corresponds to the one that would later be placed on his tomb. He also includes here that he was born at 8:44 on the morning of 8 February 1577, at the latitude of 52 degrees, 30 minutes, the position of Lindley given elsewhere in the volume. The volume also contains a note to an unpublished passage of Simon Forman that lends support to the possibility that Burton knew him and had been treated for melancholy by him as a young man.[36] This handbook and the other works on judicial astrology in Burton's library indicate a serious and lifelong interest in the subject, an interest contrasting somewhat with the more noncommittal attitude he exhibits in the *Anatomy*. Though he there appears cautiously to approve the use of astrology in medicine (2.1.4.1), in other passages he reprobates the belief that the stars rule human events. Probably his most considered answer is given in his discussion of whether the stars may cause melancholy:

If thou shalt ask me what I think, I must answer, *nam et doctis hisce erroribus versatus sum* [for I too am conversant with these learned errors], they do incline, but not compel; no necessity at all, *agunt non cogunt:* and so gently incline, that a wise man may resist them; *sapiens dominabitur astris* [a wise man will rule his stars]; they rule us, but God rules them. (1.2.1.4; 1.206)

Burton here takes a measured public position, one consistent with his status as a clergyman of the Church of England.[37] It does not betray the fact that privately he was very much inclined to seek what could be learned from the stars, a knowledge that may not determine one's fate or character but nevertheless should be understood as seriously molding his temperament and physical constitution.

Another well-used book in Burton's library may bring to mind the anecdote told of him a century later, probably apocryphal and based on what Burton himself says of Democritus in the *Anatomy*, that for amusement he would walk down to the river to hear the bargemen "scold and storm and swear at one another."[38] (The Thames, unfortunately, was not navigable by barges as far as Oxford until the last few years of Burton's life.) Whatever the status of the story,

Burton's copy of Thomas Dekker's *The Belman of London* (1608) points to an interest not entirely dissimilar from such pleasures. The book is a satiric description of rogues and thieves, one of a series Dekker wrote. But it was not so much the moral point as the object itself of the satire that captured Burton's interest, and he compiled his own sizable glossary of terms from the cant dialect of London low life, a dictionary of thieves' and beggars' argot with English translations. Was such popular philology a hobby of Burton's? Was he comparing London street slang with what he had collected in the sizable market town that Oxford was? Does the anecdote about his enjoying the quarrelsome bargemen represent an inexact record of this interest? His fondness in the *Anatomy* for slang and odd colloquialisms suggest just such a fascination with the vulgar side of the vulgar tongue.

Burton's books can also tell us something of his habits as a reader. It is not true, as has sometimes been suggested, that Burton rarely annotated his books and depended entirely on his memory. He did not make systematic notes, and some of his books have no markings, but he frequently reminded himself of passages he found significant with lines in the margin, underscoring, or a marginal word to label the subject. Very occasionally he offered an opinion of an author, as when he wrote in the margin of a book by Johannes Leo Placentius, "qui fecit hunc librum fuit illiteratus asinus" [the author of this book is an illiterate ass]. When after only a few pages of his book on "the madnesse of astrologers" George Carleton concludes "that Judiciarie Astrologie is a superstitiuous Vanity," Burton demands marginally, "What alreadie?" But his library provides no clue to a system he might have used to keep track of his immense reading. The closest we get are occasional lists he would sometimes leave on the back of a title page or in the endpapers of other writers on the same subject. At the conclusion of a dialogue on laughter by Antonius Laurentius (1606) Burton records three other writers on the subject. On the flyleaf of Johannes Garceus's *Astrologiae Methodus* (in a Basel edition of 1576) he lists some forty authors and titles of what he considers the best works on judicial astrology, especially nativities, that he has read. A book that Burton may have mined for quotations, rather as if it were a florilegium or dictionary of classical commonplaces, is Georgius Thomson's *Vindex Veritatis, Adversus Justum Lipsium* (1606). The book contains hundreds of quotations from classical authors, church fathers, and more recent theologians, and these Burton marked with his pen, occasionally labeling them by subject. But this is as close as we get—and admittedly not very close—to seeing the prodigious author of the *Anatomy* in the reader of these books. If Burton had a system that enabled him to marshall his learning for his book, it has not survived in his library.

Life beyond the Library

Another post Burton held a decade before he became librarian of Christ Church causes us to see him in a very different light. On 10 October 1615 he was named, with one Evarard Chambers, one of the clerks of the Market of Oxford. The two of them were reappointed the following year, and Burton served again, with a Thomas Crane, in 1618.[39] The clerks of the market were responsible for testing the weights and measures of the vendors and for forbidding the sale of spoiled meat and fish, butter and cheese, wine and ale. Fines were levied against offenders. We needn't suppose that Burton, like Adam Overdo in *Bartholemew Fair*, lurked about every market day smelling the fish and sampling the ale. Perhaps some of the enforcement was done by deputy or in response to complaints. But three terms of service argues a successful fulfilling of this town-gown post of authority very different from his usual tutorial duties. A Burton acquainted with the marketing practices of the fishmongers and brewers of Oxford suggests a worldliness at some variance with his self-portrait in the *Anatomy* of a scholar mewed up in his books.

When Burton was awarded the degree of bachelor of divinity on 16 May 1614, he became eligible for ordination and preferment to a church living. The opportunity came two and a half years later when the living of St. Thomas in the suburbs of Oxford fell vacant by the death of the previous incumbent. Since the Reformation the vicarage of St. Thomas was in the patronage of Christ Church and had been served by one of its members. On 29 November 1616 Burton was presented to the living by the Dean and Chapter of Christ Church, a position he held until his death.[40] St. Thomas was a pleasant ten- or fifteen-minute walk through country lanes from Christ Church. It is hard to say what impression the learned Mr. Burton of Christ Church left on his rural congregation, but he left a mark on the small Gothic church which is still to be seen. In

1621 he rebuilt the south porch and above the door placed his family arms, the shield with three dogs' heads, and below that the date and a sundial. The one other memorial of his pastorship is Anthony à Wood's record that he always gave his parishioners the sacrament in wafers. This was evidence of High-Church sympathy worth noting in the 1620s and 1630s.[41]

Burton's second piece of ecclesiastical preferment came in 1624 when he received the rectorship of Walesby in Lincolnshire. In his "Digression of Air" he mentions Walesby, "where I lately received a real kindness, by the munificence of the Right Honorable my noble Lady and Patroness, the Lady Frances, Countess Dowager of Exeter" (2.2.3;2:68; added in 1628 ed.). Though he must have visited it, he appears never to have been in residence, for all the parish records are signed by his curate, Thomas Benson.[42] But Burton benefited the living (and himself) if not the parish, for through the episcopal court of Lincoln he won back nine acres of land that had been taken away by Lady Frances's predecessor as patron.[43] In the 1632 edition of the *Anatomy* Burton appended a note to his reference to Walesby: "Lately resigned for some special reasons." Pressure to resign may have been brought on Burton so that Lionel Cranfield, earl of Middlesex and a friend of Lady Frances, could present someone else to the living. If so, Burton's terse note needn't necessarily reflect bitterness. In the *Anatomy* he shows a certain ambivalence about his experience with patrons, always discontented at not having received enough from them, but not entirely sure that it isn't his own fault for not having exerted himself and sued more openly. But even when he slips into Latin to express his dissatisfaction more feelingly, he sets Lady Frances and Lord Berkeley among his "bountiful patrons and noble benefactors" (2.3.7;2:188–89). It seems possible that Burton's resignation in 1631 was part of some amicable settlement of benefit also to him.

In any case Burton was at this point on the verge of receiving the most valuable piece of preferment he would hold during his lifetime, the living of Seagrave in Leicestershire. His shrewdness in securing the rectorship has recently come to light.[44] Some eight years earlier, on 3 September 1624, George Lord Berkeley, to whom the *Anatomy* had been dedicated in 1621, granted Burton the advowson, or the right of presentation, of the living in Seagrave. Three days later Burton assigned this interest in the advowson to his brothers William and George and to his cousin George Purfoy of

Wadley, Berkshire, with the intent that they should present him
"or some other person unto the said benefice." Berkeley wished to
reward Burton with the handsome living of Seagrave, but because
the living was not vacant, gave him instead the advowson, or right
to present a rector to it. Because the holder of the advowson could
not present himself, Burton then assigned it to three trustworthy
relatives who would be certain to present him when the living fell
vacant. In this way he would not have to depend on anything so
fragile as a lord's promise of preferment. Burton likely worked this
scheme out for himself, perhaps with his brother William's legal
advice. On 10 June 1632 Edward Cooper, the old rector of Seagrave,
was buried by his curate. The Burtons lost no time. By a deed of
15 June 1632 William and George presented Robert to the living,
and on 25 June he was inducted into it, that is, given full control
of his parish and the legal rights to its income. Again the bookish
scholar proved a keen man of affairs.

It was not until age fifty-five, then, when he would have less
than eight years to enjoy it, that Burton held a living which he
would have considered at all worthy of his accomplishments. Besides
its income, Seagrave had for him the advantage of being only a day's
journey, some twenty miles, beyond Lindley, so he might combine
family visiting with attention to pastoral duty. But a curate was
still necessary, and it was through his curate that Burton paid in
peace of mind for the income Seagrave brought. He employed John
Mallinson, a rash young graduate (1630) of Magdalen College. Shortly
after assuming his curacy, Mallinson accused the wife of one of the
leading families of his parish of adultery.[45] He alleged that Mary
Reade, wife of William Reade, a prosperous farmer, had let a certain
Thomas Fielding into her dairy house at night and covered the
window with her apron. Six years later, after the death of her
husband, Mary Reade would bring a libel suit against Mallinson
for his accusation, stating that by his "defamatory and scandalous
words" he had implied she had "committed that foule sinne of
adultery or fornicacion, and that thereby she was a common whore
and an incontinent person." Any quarrel by the curate was bound
to embroil the rector, and by 1635 Burton was writing to Berkeley's
steward, John Smyth, a lawyer and himself a scholar, to ask him
to prevent William Reade from ploughing up a field he intended
to lease from the rector.[46] Burton protests that this is the field where
he pastures his horses when he comes to Seagrave, and if he has no

hay there, he will have to pay Reade for pasture, who has already charged him more for an overgrazed field than he pays for hay in Oxford. He plays upon the sense of shared interest among scholars and implies that his dignity is injured by this quarrel with Reade: "I am my Lordes servant and obsequious Chaplin, and he a Bayley, let me not be insulted or tyrannised over, so iniuriously abused by a Farmer." He refers to other journeys he has had to make over the matter and how he has been "otherwise abused by this partye, and y^t in grosse and saucye manner." No record exists of how the matter came out, whether the rector saved his pasture or the widow won her libel suit, but it is obvious that Burton was not allowed a quiet enjoyment of the preferment he had waited for so long.

Conspicuous by its absence among Burton's references to the clerical profession in the *Anatomy* is any expression of his sense of the spiritual dimension of the priesthood. In stark contrast to George Herbert, another learned university man who assumed a clerical living in the early 1630s, Burton never speaks of the awesome responsibility of preaching the gospel or ministering the sacraments to his parishioners. He does not seem troubled by questions of spiritual worthiness or how the Old Adam may assume the priesthood of the New. Silence need not mean indifference to such matters, but when Burton does speak of the clerical life, it is entirely in terms of a reward, inadequate, tardy, and tedious, for the accomplishments of the scholar. As early as the first edition of the *Anatomy* in 1621, when he had spent five years as vicar of St. Thomas, he described the parson's life as poor compensation for the rigors of university life: "If after long expectation and much earnest suit of our selves and friends we obtaine a small benefice at last: our misery begins afresh, we light upon a crackt title, or stand in feare of some precedent lapse, or some litigious people, that will not pay their dues without repining, or compelled by long suit . . . and put case they be quiet honest men, make the best of it, as often falls out, he must turne rusticke, and dayly conuerse with a company of Idiots and Clownes" (1621 ed., 186). Three years later Burton expanded this passage considerably to expatiate on the miseries the parson faced: a ruinous rectory that must be repaired, the necessity of suing for dilapidations (or be sued himself by his successor), his predecessor's arrearages, the sectarians, Puritans, papists, or "atheistical epicures" in his parish (1.2.3.15;1:323). Except for the troublesome parishioners, all the miseries are economic. Since Burton had not yet received Walesby and as vicar of St. Thomas lived in college, he is not speaking from bitter experience of the ills attendant on taking a benefice. But his conclusion does not suggest that he had found, or could even imagine, much spiritual reward in dealing with the poor and humble of his parish. In the 1624 edition he did add, in his utopian vision (Democritus Junior to the Reader, 1:102), that he "would have such priests as should imitate Christ." But the Old Adam worried about dilapidations and tithes and preferred the conversation of the senior common room. As a churchman Burton is likely to remind us of one of Trollope's more worldly clergymen.

But if he was not possessed of the spiritual resources that characterized the best of his contemporaries, we must suppose that he was prompt and dutiful in fulfilling his clerical responsibilities. In his will he made a donation to his parish at Seagrave, "as I have lately done to St. Thomas's parish." Burton was a man who recognized obligations. Wood says he was accounted by those who knew him well "a person of great honesty, plain dealing and charity."[47] Unlike many of his contemporaries, he published none of his sermons, and in "Democritus to the Reader" says rather scornfully that he has been "as desirous to suppress my labors in this kind as others to publish theirs" (1:35). In *Philosophaster* the false theologian was until recently a rhetorician who could wield heavy words and "thrill the very goddess of Persuasion to the marrow."[48] In an age when preaching was much valued, Burton apparently did not cultivate a reputation as a preacher. No doubt he did preach, and the *Anatomy* contains sermons of a kind, but on the basis of these we can only guess that he impressed his learned auditors with the breadth of his scholarship and left the unlearned to exercise the virtue of patience. The rural members of his parishes must have viewed the scholarly Mr. Burton as a somewhat remote figure, perhaps rather shy with them, punctilious in fulfilling his duties and asking the same of them. We may infer that he expected his tithes to be paid on time, but could be charitable enough in cases of real need.

The *Anatomy* and the Hope of Reward

Burton's character as a clergyman points up a central fact about him: although he was by training and profession a divine, the central work of his life was *The Anatomy of Melancholy*. The book is what absorbed him, and to it he gave his greatest energies. The *Anatomy* was, finally, his calling. If pressed, he might have replied that his real ministry was to bring comfort through the book to those suffering melancholy. "It is a disease of the soul on which I am to treat," he says in anticipation of such an objection, "and as much appertaining to a divine as to a physician, and who knows not what an agreement there is betwixt these two professions?" (Democritus to the Reader, 1:37). A good divine should be a good physician, "as our Saviour calls Himself, and was indeed." Because melancholy is the rock on which he was himself "fatally driven," so he will turn his hand to ministering to other sufferers.

We have no way of knowing when Burton began writing the *Anatomy*. Perhaps he began his researches to find relief for himself while still in his twenties. Probably the idea of a book grew gradually as he gathered material. By the time Burton was in his middle thirties, the book must have been well begun, and after the completion of his divinity degree at age thirty-seven, he was able to devote full attention to it. He signs his "Conclusion to the Reader," which appeared only in the first edition, "From my Studie in Christ Church Oxon. Decemb. 5. 1620." Except for contributions of verses to various Oxford volumes commemorating royal visits, births, marriages, and deaths, this was the forty-three-year-old author's first publication.

The *Anatomy* apparently sold well from the beginning. Wood says that Burton's publisher, Henry Cripps, "got an estate by it." But if we judge the success of the first edition by the only criterion that mattered in the seventeenth century, patronage, it was a failure in its author's eyes. Burton dedicated the book to the young George Lord Berkeley, but as we have seen, Berkeley did not grant the advowson of Seagrave to Burton until 1624, at the time the second edition appeared. The failure to obtain immediate patronage by his book must have been a bitter pill for Burton to swallow. Even in the first edition he gives ample indication of his feelings that he is long overdue for preferment. "No labour in the world like unto study," he exclaims in calling attention to the "many diseases of body and mind" a scholar must endure.

It may be, their temperature will not endure it, but in striving to be excellent, to know all, they loose health, wealth, wit, life and all. Let him yet happily escape all these hazards, and is now consummate and ripe, he hath profitted in his studies, and proceeded with all applause, after many expenses, he is now fit for preferment, where shall he have it? he is as farre to seek as he was (after twenty years standing) as the first day of his coming to the University. (1621 ed., 173; 1.2.3.15;1:306).

It had been twenty-seven years since Burton's first day at the university, twenty-one since he entered Christ Church. Clearly the vicarage of St. Thomas was insufficient to compensate his merit and toil. His chapter on the miseries of scholars is peppered by several such reflections on neglected and ill-compensated scholars. But even with publication of the *Anatomy*, with its formal dedication to Berkeley, nothing further, as it appeared, was forthcoming. In the second edition most of these passages are amplified in ways that make Burton's bitterness evident. Perhaps the most telling addition in 1624 is in the chapter that shows him fighting a losing battle "Against Envy, Livor, Emulation, Hatred, Ambition, Self-love and all other affections" (2.3.6;2:186). In 1621 he had admitted that he "was once so mad to bussell abroad, & seeke about for preferment, tire myself and trouble all my friends." Now three years later he slips into Latin to add:

but I gained nothing from all my labour. Some of my friends died, others would no longer know me, others even hated me; some made liberal promises and even pretended to intercede actively on my behalf and fed me with false hopes; so while I paid court to some and won over others and made myself known, I began to get on in years, time flowed on, my friends grew tired and I was constantly put off, until weary of the world and sick of the faithlessness of men, I gave up the struggle. (2.3.6;2:188)

From this we can conjecture that Lord Berkeley had promised a reward for the dedication of the *Anatomy*, but had not as yet delivered. (This would also explain why, when the advowson was finally offered, Burton followed the shrewd course he did instead of trusting to a promise.) In the third edition of 1628 he acknowledges what he has received from Berkeley and the Countess of Exeter. But his discontent keeps him from removing the Latin passage or any of his other bitter reflections on neglect.

There is a basic contradiction between Burton's hope of compensation and his scholarly occupation, a contradiction that comes of the system of academic reward in the century but that encompasses his own character as well. The only substantial reward for a university scholar in orders was ecclesiastical preferment. But a benefice meant that the possessor either held it in nonresidence through a curate or left the university and its libraries to take up residence. The first course thwarted the goal of getting an able and scholarly man to serve as pastor of a parish, and the second ended a scholarly career, or at least made its pursuit substantially more difficult. One may also wonder whether university scholars in fact made the best parish clergy, a question that intrudes in Burton's particular case. In the 1628 edition he added a wish-fulfillment tale that unintentionally raises this issue. From Valentinus Andrea he tells of twelve suitors for "a fat Prebend" in a cathedral church (2.3.7;2:191–92). The first eleven appear to have various claims of interest or alliance on the prebend—money, nobility, connection to the bishop, etc.—or of need. The fifth suitor may seem to us the only one with a claim based on professional fitness, "a painful preacher, and he was commended by the whole parish where he dwelt, and he had all their hands to his certificate." Burton's hero, however, is not this man but rather the twelfth, a suitor "only in conceit," whose description assumes a recognizable cast: "a right honest, civil, sober man, an excellent scholar, and such a one as lived private in the university, but he had neither means nor money to compass it; besides he hated all such courses, he could not speak for himself, neither had he any friends to solicit his cause, and therefore made no suit, could not expect, neither did he hope for, or look after it" (2:192). To everyone's astonishment (some said it was a miracle) the bishop chose the scholar for the prebend. "But alas!" Burton concludes gloomily, "it is but a tale, a mere fiction." Although there is no doubt in Burton's mind that an academic of proven scholarship and ability should receive ecclesiastical office, we may instead wonder that the good preacher and successful pastor was passed over in his favor. Burton complains frequently about simony in the church, but he never questions the system by which ecclesiastical office was used as a temporal reward for university scholars.

In Burton's case, however, the heart of the matter is the difficulty we have in imagining him separated from the libraries of Oxford. His ambitions clearly exceeded a benefice he could hold in absentia. In the passage he added to thank his patrons in 1628 he appears to be fighting these ambitions with indifferent success: "I may not deny but that I have had some bountiful patrons and noble benefactors, *ne sim interim ingratus,* and I do thankfully acknowledge it,

I have received some kindness . . . more peradventure than I deserve, though not to my desire, more of them than I did expect, yet not of others to my desert; neither am I ambitious or covetous all this while, or a Suffenus unto myself; what I have said, without prejudice or alteration shall stand" (2.3.7;2:189). What he has said are the bitter Latin words, added in 1624 and never canceled, about the broken promises of patrons and the failure of his hopes of preferment. In part no doubt he is illustrating the discontent against which he is supplying the remedy. But the language here zigzags curiously between acknowledgment of actual benefits and dissatisfaction that he has not received more. We may guess that Burton felt himself entitled to a cathedral deanery, or perhaps even a bishopric. But such offices as these could not have been held as sinecures from the Bodleian or Christ Church libraries. His appetite for books, to say nothing of the augmentation of the *Anatomy,* could hardly have been fed solely by his own library. Although he could finally tell himself in the last edition printed in his lifetime, "I had as lief be still Democritus Junior" than a doctor or a lord bishop (1.2.3.15;1:314), he was torn for most of his life between these ambitions and the university life that obviously suited him.

Dissatisfaction ran deep in Burton. Its expression ranges from the offhand comment that although he delights in the country, he may not have such a life (2.2.4;2:79) to his sharp attack on the university that concludes his disquisition on the miseries of scholars (1.2.3.15;1:324–30). The latter, in fact, reveals the ways Burton may have insured that his ambitions would remain frustrated. He again slips into Latin to protect his denunciation from the eyes of the unlearned. But it was hardly the unlearned whom it would most offend. What is significant is that the attack was not added in a later edition out of frustration or dissatisfaction at identifiable circumstances, but filled three and a half pages of the first edition. In 1624 he added particularly barbed sallies at "some of those who sit at the helm," charging that they advanced not by merit but by simony. Nor did he ever retract or soften the charges.

He assigns responsibility for the political evils of the state to the university: ill-educated and completely unqualified students were being awarded degrees; the heads of the university were keeping up enrollments strictly for financial gain; indeed, both university and church were filled with veniality and corruption. "Meanwhile learned men, graced with all the distinctions of a holy life, and who bear the heat of the day, are condemned by a hard fate to serve these men, content perhaps with a scanty salary, without any titles to their names, humble and obscure, though eminently worthy, and so, needy and unhonoured, they lead a retired life, buried in some poor benefice or imprisoned forever in their college chambers, where they languish in obscurity" (1.2.3.15;1:330). It is one thing to attack the university when one is safely out of it, but to take aim, as Burton does, at the institution and its governors when all one's advancement depends upon them, argues a desire, at some level, to fulfill his most pessimistic prophecies. Burton seems determined to be, in spite of himself, the obscure and neglected man of learning he so frequently sketches.

It is in this respect, I think, that the *Anatomy* can be seen as a book Burton was writing for himself as well as for the malcontent melancholiacs of the world at large. Just as much of its paradoxical and self-contradictory character comes of the complexity of its author's personality, so too are the sermons and exhortations to contentment directed toward himself. Burton appears at times to offer himself as an example of the ills he deplores, then to argue himself into submission in a curious blend of self-accusation and self-justification. The *Anatomy,* more than any book one can think of, is a monument to and expression of the solitary and endless pleasures of reading, searching, and comparing. But it never itself achieves any serenity about this activity, either about the results it may attain to or its value in comparison with other activities. The melancholy against which Burton fought was a restless, dissatisfied, malcontented state of mind.

Wood says of Burton that "he was by many accounted a severe student, a devourer of authors, a melancholy and humorous [that is, eccentric and moody] person." His acerbity toward the university and his dissatisfaction with his own position may well have translated into a public reputation for being formidable and difficult, a man who preferred the company of his books and whose shyness seemed arrogance. But his intimates, Wood reports, knew another side of him: "I have heard some of the ancients of Ch. Ch. often say that his company was very merry, facete and juvenile, and no man in his time did surpass him for his ready and dextrous interlarding his common discourses among them with verses from the poets or sentences from the classical authors."[49] And this, of course, is the other side of the *Anatomy,* delight in the comic variability of men's opinions and pleasure in the words that express them. Though he had trouble reconciling himself to it, Burton finally knew that he belonged amid libraries and books, that he "had as lief be still Democritus Junior," and to this end, even in spite of himself, he organized his life. The sense of Burton we draw from passages concerned with preferment and thwarted ambition must be balanced against chapters like the "Digression of Air." Books were his life; through them he was able to emerge from himself and encounter a greater world he would not otherwise know. In its variety and multiplicity the world of the library may entangle its inhabitant and induce the melancholy of skepticism. But this is a larger, more capacious melancholy, one with room for laughter, beyond the melancholy of self-absorbed discontent.

The Death that Melancholy Gave

On 15 August 1639 some five months before his death, Burton drew up his last will and testament.[50] Although he says he is "at this present I thank God in perfect health of Bodie and Mind," the language may be more conventional than literal since wills at the time were commonly drafted when death was felt to be close, generally a few months before the fact.[51] But Burton, as we shall see, may have been both in perfect health of body and mind *and* persuaded that death was close. His will contains no surprising revelations about his character or life, but it does illustrate several facets well. It shows in the first instance his family feeling. He gives the land his father had willed him to his older brother William and his heirs, thereby consolidating the Burton estate. The income from the land he divides principally between his nephew Cassibelane, William's son, and his only living sister, Catherine. All of his other living relatives are named as beneficiaries, probably according to what he thought were their various needs. He provides dutifully for his servant John Upton, both an annuity of 40 shillings and a gift of the same amount, and 40 shillings for the servants of Christ Church. Similarly, he leaves five pounds for the parish of Seagrave, as he says he has recently done for St. Thomas. The charity Wood remarks emerges in various small gifts to the poor of the places where he had spent portions of his life, at Nuneaton "where I was once a Grammar Scholar," at Higham "where my land is," and at St. Thomas parish. He remembers Brasenose with a gift of five pounds to the library. But as we might expect, his major beneficiaries, after his relatives, are the libraries where he spent his life at Oxford, a hundred pounds each to the Bodleian and the Christ Church libraries, specifying that the money was to go for land yielding five pounds a year. In this way he hoped to restock the shelves of his old haunts in perpetuity. His more valuable and lasting legacy to them was almost an afterthought: "If I have any books the University Library hath not let them take them[;] If I have any Books our own Library hath not let them take them." In practice this meant that John Rouse, Burton's friend and the librarian of the Bodleian, went through his books several months later and chose about half of them, mainly the sort of books Thomas Bodley had excluded thirty-five years before. The remainder, except the ones specified as gifts in the will, went to Christ Church. In addition he made small gifts to various friends and colleagues. The will suggests that his closest friends at the end of his life were the family of Dr. Samuel Fell, the high church Dean of Christ Church, for he gives his "English books of Husbandry" to Mrs. Fell, his six pieces of silver plate and spoons to their daughter Catherine, and most of his mathematical instruments to their son John, the future dean of Christ Church and bishop of Oxford.

Death seems not to have come suddenly to Burton, for the will contains the note that it was shown and acknowledged to John Morris, the treasurer of Christ Church, "some few days before his death." He died on 25 January 1640, just two weeks before his sixty-third birthday, and was buried two days later in the north aisle of Christ Church Cathedral. Whatever the actual cause of death, his fame as a melancholic and astrologer made him a mark for gossip in the college. John Aubrey, who was writing in the second half of the seventeenth century, reports that "Mr. Robert Hooke of Gresham's College told me that he lay in the chamber in Christ Church that was Mr. Burton's of whom 'tis whispered that, *non obstante* all his astrologie and his booke of Melancholie, he ended his dayes in that chamber by hanging him selfe."[52] Wood also mentions the conjecture: "R. Burton paid his last debt to nature, in his chamber in Ch. Ch. at, or very near that time, which he had some years before foretold from the calculation of his own nativity. Which being exact, several of the students did not forebear to whisper among themselves, that rather than there should be a mistake in the calculation, he sent up his soul to heaven thro' a slip about his neck."[53]

The gossip may also have arisen in part from Burton's apparently lenient discussion of suicide in the *Anatomy* (1.4.1;1:431–39). But the lenience expressed there is in judgment of the victim, not toward the act itself. Burton records classical writers' approval of suicide in certain circumstances before turning, in perfectly orthodox fashion, to Christian disapprobations of it. The discussion, in any case, does not sound like the argument of a man talking himself into suicide or rationalizing it in anticipation. The circumstances of his burial, however, are the principal witness against the student gossip; a suicide would not have been permitted Christian burial, let alone in so honored a location. Burton's brother William erected a monument to him and placed on it the witty Latin epitaph Burton composed for himself: "Paucis notus, paucioribus ignotus, hic jacet Democritus Junior, cui vitam dedit et mortem Melancholia" (Known to few [as Burton], unknown to fewer [as Democritus Junior], here lies Democritus Junior, to whom Melancholy gave life and death). If the death that melancholy gave could be thought to hint at suicide, the hint, as Nochimson points out, was not strong enough to keep William from placing it on the tomb.[54] "Burton's Melancholy," moreover, was the way by which his book was known in the seventeenth century, so the *Melancholia* of the epitaph refers not only to a disease, but to his life-absorbing work.[55] Nor does the document by which we know the date of Burton's death give any indication of other than natural causes; the vice-chancellor of the university, Accepted Frewen, wrote to the chancellor, Archbishop Laud: "On Saturday Jan. 25, died Mr. Robert Burton of Christ Church, who hath given £ 5. *per annum* for ever to the University Library, besides a considerable number of books to be taken out of his studie; and because a benefactor to the University, I was present at his funeral."[56]

Burton's death need not have been suicide to have been strongly influenced by astrological calculations based on his nativity. The heavenly signs clearly indicated a physical crisis at the close of his sixty-third year.[57] Indeed the planets were in such dangerous and unfavorable aspects, some indeed portending a violent death, that Burton could scarcely have hoped to see his birthday. We don't have to believe in astrology ourselves to understand the effect these calculations must have had on a sensitive mind that was persuaded of the stars' influence. The astrological picture Vicari sketches—

and that Burton sketched for himself—would go some way toward scaring an adept to death, or toward bringing on a crisis of a preexistent condition. And Burton was, as we have seen, sufficiently persuaded of his danger to have made out his will some months before. That done, he may simply have resigned himself to await the death he believed would come just before he entered his sixty-fourth year.

The monument William erected has a rather wooden-looking colored bust above the epitaph. To the left stands a stylized copy of Burton's nativity, that emblem of melancholy that proved such an accurate—or self-fulfilling—prognostic of his life. To the right is a curious geometric figure that probably signifies his interest in mathematics and cosmology. Above are the family arms, the same three dogs' heads on a blue ground he had placed above the porch of St. Thomas Church. The date of death on the monument, "VIII Id Ian. AC MDCXXXIX," i.e., 6 January 1639, is wrong, perhaps an error for VIII Kal Feb. (25 January). (The year, of course, is Old Style, since the new year was still dated from 25 March.) But the most notable feature of the monument is the riddling epitaph, with no name but that of his bookish persona, Democritus Junior. One may imagine that the shy and ironic Burton would approve of the way it still speaks only to the knowing.

If we are unpersuaded that the bust on the tomb conveys much of the Democritus Junior who was known and unknown, we can turn instead to the portrait of him in Brasenose College. The date on it is also wrong. It says he was sixty-two when it was painted in 1635; in fact he was fifty-eight. But no matter. There we see a man in academic garb looking up from the book open on a cushion before him. The clipped beard and starched ruff suggest the fastidious and careful man of learning. But the revealing features are the clear eyes and the pursed lips. They convey a sense of detached amusement at what he has just read, as if he knows scores of instances that both confirm and contradict his author.

Chapter Two

Melancholy and
the Printed Word

Burton's *Anatomy of Melancholy* poses us an immediate problem of
definition. What is this expansive, twelve-hundred-page book that
begins with a seriocomic apology for itself and ends with a sermon
of quotations emphasizing God's mercy? What can an author intend
who initially conceals himself in the mask of Democritus, the laughing philosopher of fifth-century Abdera, then in the course of the
book reveals himself to us as a discontented, melancholic don clois-
tered in the libraries of Oxford? Are we to take the book as a scientific
study of melancholy (we would say depression) in its dissection of
the subject through partitions, sections, members, and subsections,
complete with elaborate outlines? Or is the *Anatomy* rather a therapeutic work for melancholiacs, a collection of advice for the afflicted
that aims at being comprehensive, the great-grandfather of that
thriving modern genre of self-help books? Or is the book's fondness
for odd lore, its frequent digressiveness, its pleasure in anecdote
and strange incident, a sign that its author means simply to entertain
us with his formidable learning?

Critical Reputation and
the Problem of Definition

The vagaries of the reputation of the *Anatomy* suggest something
of this problem of definition. The popularity both of melancholy
and of its *Anatomy* in the seventeenth century points to the book's
original therapeutic use. If every age can be said to have its characteristic psychic illness, melancholy was the affliction that beset,
and distinguished, Renaissance men and women. The *Anatomy*, from
its first publication in 1621 until 1676, went through eight editions. Burton had compiled all that was known about melancholy,
a virtual encyclopedia of the disease, and readers bought up the
book for its use to them in overcoming their sufferings. At the end

34

of the first section, after he has distinguished melancholy from other mental disorders and anatomized the faculties of the human soul, he says he will treat melancholy so "that every man that is in any measure affected with this malady may know how to examine it in himself, and apply remedies unto it" (1.1.3.4;1:176). Melancholy readers, of course, found it a mine of advice, from the most particular prescriptions for herbal remedies to general moral and spiritual counsel. As long as melancholy was understood in the ways Renaissance medicine defined it, the *Anatomy* had a genuine therapeutic claim.[1]

Then the book went into eclipse for a century and a quarter, not finding its way into print again until 1800. In the last quarter of the seventeenth century and throughout the eighteenth century the *Anatomy* was valued less as a book to be read than as a repository of learning and quotations. Anthony à Wood, writing in the 1690s, calls it "a book so full of variety of reading, that gentlemen who have lost their time and are put to a push for invention, may furnish themselves with matter for common or scholastical discourse and writing."[2] He adds that several writers "have unmercifully stolen matter from the said book without any acknowledgment," and he goes on to name one such plagiarist. Another was Sterne, whose thieveries in *Tristam Shandy* went undetected for some thirty years until John Ferrier pointed them out in his *Illustration of Sterne* in 1798.[3] An exception to this tendency to leave Burton on the shelf until one needed a tag of Latin was Dr. Johnson, who said it was "the only book that ever took him out of bed two hours sooner than he wished to rise."[4] Was it pleasure in Burton's learning that commended him to Johnson, or did he, as a sufferer himself from melancholy, use him for the therapeutic purposes Burton intended?

For the Romantics, and especially Charles Lamb, the *Anatomy* became a book whose only purpose was to entertain with its curious, long-forgotten learning, its tales, and digressions. The *Anatomy* became an antique, literally so in Lamb's preference that it should be read in a seventeenth-century folio and not in the quarto of 1800. To Lamb, Burton was "a fantastic old great man" who had combed the shelves of ancient libraries and filled his book with his antiquarian lore. Burton's colloquial style also appealed to the Romantics, and Lamb parodied it lovingly. Their enthusiasm led to a revival of interest in the *Anatomy* in the nineteenth century—more than forty editions were published—and more than anything else con-

tributed to the modern sense that the book should be known and
praised, if at a cautious distance. To the early twentieth century,
in reaction, was left the reassertion of the *Anatomy*'s seriousness and
scientific purpose. Sir William Osler, himself a physician, called it
"the greatest medical treatise written by a layman." In *The Psychiatry
of Robert Burton* Bergen Evans, in consultation with a modern psy-
chiatrist, attempted to evaluate Burton's psychology in the light of
modern psychoanalytical practice. William R. Mueller found in the
Anatomy serious analysis of the economic, political, social, and religious problems of its age.[5]

There are difficulties—as well as truth—in each of these ways
the *Anatomy* has been understood, and it is not so much with the
hope of arriving at the final truth as of expressing the complexity
of the problem of definition that I mention them. The one concept
that more recent criticism has been unable to dispense with in
discussing the *Anatomy* is paradox. To Rosalie Colie the book is a
"structure of paradox" in which various genres, some mutually contradictory, are brought together in a whole that is conscious of its
paradoxical nature. Joan Webber calls attention to the unstable,
constantly shifting sense Burton creates of his own literary self in
the persona of Democritus. Stanley Fish reads the *Anatomy* as the
most conclusively "self-consuming artifact" produced by a self-consuming age, a book designed to illustrate to a reader the contradictions in its own discourse. Ruth Fox's sustained and careful
reading of the structure of the *Anatomy* sees it as a book paradoxically
attempting to balance order and disorder, to portray as fully as
possible the disordered state of humanity.[6] Having learned from
these critics and sharing the critical assumptions of our age, I find
myself similarly unable to dispense with the idea of paradox in
thinking about Burton. There is no denying that the *Anatomy* was
a strange, original sort of book when it first appeared, and it has
remained just as strange after three and a half centuries of being
read, interpreted, and pilfered from. Nothing one can say about it
goes unqualified or unchallenged.

To begin with its therapeutic claims, one might point out that
several of its predecessors offer more immediately useful advice for
the sufferer. Timothy Bright's *Treatise of Melancholy* (1586), for
example, helpfully distinguishes between melancholy and religious
despair and has, moreover, a tone of sympathetic concern and encouragement that Burton never matches. André Du Laurens's treat-

ment of melancholy (1594), probably the closest of Burton's sources, is altogether clearer and more straightforward in describing the disease and saying what can be done for it.[7] But even in its own terms the *Anatomy* confronts its reader with problems in its therapeutic aims. No remedy or prescription is ever tendered with confident authority—or frequently even commended as preferable to the dozens of other remedies listed. And seldom is any advice uncontradicted by other advice coming within a few pages. Even the book's intention of providing therapy for melancholy is rendered problematic when Burton, quoting Damascenus out of Penottus, advises us "that, without exquisite knowledge, to work out of books is most dangerous: how unsavory a thing it is to believe writers, and take upon trust" (2.1.4.2;2:20). And lest we suspect some complicated irony in such bookish advice against trusting books, like St. Paul's paradox of a Cretan calling all Cretans liars, Burton adds that a friend of his nearly poisoned himself when he tried a prescription of hellebore he had found in a book. He is also well aware of the perils of intern's disease. "Some young physicians, that studying to cure diseases," he notes, "catch them themselves, will be sick, and appropriate all symptoms they find related of others to their own persons" (1.3.1.2;1:388). So the best advice he can give to the melancholiac is "not to read this tract of Symptoms, lest he disquiet or make himself for a time worse, and more melancholy than he was before." This is one self-help book honest enough to admit that it may not work, that parts of it may even aggravate the malady. Yet for page after page the examination of the disease and the search for a remedy go on.

As a scientific study of melancholy, the *Anatomy* presents at least as many problems. In spite of the apparatus of analysis in its synoptic tables, a reader soon realizes that Burton is in many ways the least analytic of writers, that he is no scientist even by the gentler canons of seventeenth-century definition. In Douglas Bush's memorable formulation, "sitting between Bacon and Hobbes, he appears as a kind of gargoyle between the two spires of the cathedral of English scientific thought."[8] Not only does Burton have no interest in the experimental, but he imposes no hierarchy upon his massive and disparate body of authorities. Hippocrates, Galen, and Averroes are there jostling with scores of more recent European writers—he calls them his "neoterics"—and no writer or school of thought ever attains to any particular authority. If he knew Freud and our neoterics, we suspect, they too would be there rubbing shoulders with the medical authorities of two thousand years and more. The seriousness Burton has been assigned by his modern commentators is surely a part of his intention. He does see melancholy as a grave psychological disorder of his time, and in its ubiquity he finds it affecting all parts of social, moral, and political life. But his understanding of these ills is so unevenly grounded in the detail of his contemporary world that there is a bookishness even about his social and moral satire. In spite of the claims made for him, he shows little engagement with economics or politics, no awareness of the contemporary contests between king and parliament. One may read the *Anatomy* without being aware that England was moving toward civil war in Burton's lifetime. No doubt Lamb and the Romantics were blind to one side of the book in stressing its quaint charm at the expense of its serious and scientific claims, but these latter claims are not the essence of the book, nor are they likely to explain readers' continuing interest in it.

Another curiosity of the *Anatomy* is that although its composition springs from Burton's own experience of melancholy—it discloses, as we have seen, a considerable amount of information about his life—it remains in the end oddly impersonal. He tells us almost immediately that he writes of melancholy to cure his own: "for I had *gravidum cor, foedum caput,* a kind of impostume in my head, which I was very desirous to be unladen of, and could imagine no fitter evacuation than this." As he expatiates on this personal genesis of his book, he admits the doubleness of the explanation. "I was not a little offended with this malady, shall I say my mistress Melancholy, my Egeria, or my *malus genius*" (Democritus Junior to the Reader; 1:21). His subject is both curse and blessing, and his book a driving out of one nail with another, "an antidote out of that which was the prime cause of my disease." Within a few sentences he drops even the mask of Democritus and refers to himself *in proprio nomine*: "Experto crede Roberto" (trust Robert who knows). "Something I can speak out of mine own experience." But he never does. What he says of melancholy comes of his learning, not of his life. For all that he is willing to include biographical details, he never draws on his own experiences of melancholy more than to acknowledge it. Burton refers to Montaigne seven times in the course of the *Anatomy,* and from him he may have taken the precedent for allowing that his subject touches his own life.[9] But unlike Montaigne, Burton never portrays his own interior experience, is never willing to let us enter his own memories or emotions.

In the middle of part 1 (1.2.3.15) Burton leads us to wonder whether his book and the labor that goes into it may not in fact be more cause than cure of his affliction. Among the causes of melancholy he includes "Love of learning, or overmuch Study," and for thirty pages he discourses feelingly on the misery of scholars. He begins by citing a dozen or more authorities to support "the common tenent of the world, that learning dulls and diminisheth the spirits, and so *per consequens* produceth melancholy" (1.2.3.15;1:301). "No labour in the world like unto study," he exclaims. "It may be their temperature will not endure it, but striving to be excellent, to know all, they lose health, wealth, wit, life, and all" (1:306). Or if a scholar has the constitution to stand it, he profits nothing by all his labor but to stay in the university as poor as when he first arrived. From this perspective the author's melancholy is more likely to be aggravated than alleviated by service to the Malady Mistress of his passion. Yet we know from reading him that Burton could no more stop writing of melancholy than he could stop reading, than he could stop quoting in Latin and citing sources, than he could cease breathing.

A Universal Anatomy

It should be obvious by now that a reader of the *Anatomy* needs a high degree of toleration for paradox, not to say inconsistency or contradiction, in approaching its perplexities. Burton himself is well aware of these inconsistencies and contradictions. In "Democritus to the Reader," which is a kind of epitome of the manner of the whole book, he exploits them for comic effect. He pretends annoyance, for example, with the potentially critical reader: "If any man take exceptions, let him turn the buckle of his girdle, I care not; I owe thee nothing (reader), I look not for favour at thy hands, I am independent, I fear not." But then, just when he has appeared to walk off in a huff, he turns on his heels and goes down on his knees: "No, I recant, I will not, I care, I fear, I confess my fault, acknowledge a great offence . . . I have overshot myself, I have spoken foolishly, rashly, unadvisedly, absurdly, I have anatomized my own folly" (1:122). But for all their comic potential, the paradoxes and contradictions are not part of an elaborate literary joke. If they were, we could reasonably object that brevity is the soul of wit and the *Anatomy* is far too long to be a plausible joke. No, Burton intends his book to be a serious discussion of a serious human problem. He is moved to do so by the universality of the disease—"few there are that feel not the smart of it" (Democritus to the Reader; 1:120). He also intends his therapeutic purposes seriously. He means, finally, what he says in his preface: "my purpose and endeavor is, in the following discourse to anatomize this humour of melancholy, through all his parts and species, as it is an habit, or an ordinary disease, and that philosophically, medicinally, to show the causes, symptoms, and several cures of it, that it may be the better avoided."

The key word here is "all." Burton aims at an encyclopedic fullness in his anatomy; he wishes to say *all* there is to say about melancholy. The seventeenth century was the last age when a man could hope to say all there was to say about a subject. In fact, this desire for encyclopedic fullness characterizes many late Renaissance works. Richard Hooker aimed to encompass all of the governance and practice of the Church in his *Laws of Ecclesiastical Polity.* Sir Walter Raleigh could attempt to write a history of the world. Michael Drayton could survey all of England in *Poly-Olbion* and plan to do the same with Scotland. Milton enfolds universal human nature into his epic of the fall of man. Burton may sound as if he is speaking hyperbolically when he describes the melancholy scholar "striving to be excellent, to know all," but from what we know of his reading, he may be speaking simply of his aspiration.

If Burton desires to report all that is known of melancholy, there is for him a further universality in the subject itself. In "Democritus to the Reader" he insists on "the necessity and generality" of melancholy: "thou shalt soon perceive that all the world is mad, that it is melancholy, dotes" (1:38–39). To speak of melancholy is to speak of humanity. Melancholy is a universal and constant in the human nature Burton sees before him. Not only the generality of mankind, but even the greatest of philosophers partake of this common foolishness, this general madness. In thus describing melancholy in his preface, Burton insures the engagement of his *Anatomy* with all of human nature; nothing human can be alien to his subject or to his book. In this sense the *Anatomy* becomes the pessimistic inverse of those high Renaissance celebrations of man's nature, works like Pico della Mirandola's *Oration on the Dignity of Man.* With another melancholiac, Burton can exclaim "What a piece of work is a man!" only to give his answer in humanity's protean capacity for folly and unhappiness. What is important to notice here is the way Burton's claim for the universality of his subject matter cuts against any scientific pretensions. The scientific study of melancholy must begin by *defining* its subject in relation to other forms of unhappiness and mental aberration. And Burton will later attempt such definition. But to turn away from definition at the outset and instead go in the opposite direction of inclusion of all that concerns human life signals the book's identification with those works of humanist universality. In Burton's aspirations the *Anatomy* is to be a book that says all that can be said about a subject that is at the center of all discourse.

Two inventions stand behind this aspiration of universality: the printed book and the library. Both inventions epitomize Renaissance humanism. The former made hundreds of unvarying copies of a text available and revolutionized not only the ways in which the written language was used but the very psychological structures through which Europeans perceived what they knew.[10] The latter invention, no less revolutionary in the ways it reordered the structures of learning, collected printed books and manuscripts together in one place so that a single reader might consult and compare them to a degree never before possible. To speak of the Renaissance invention of so ancient an institution as the library needs some justification, for obviously libraries had existed since the ancient world. But between the founding of the Vatican Library by Pope Nicholas V in the 1450s, just on the verge of the invention of printing, and the opening of the Bodleian Library a century and a half later, the institution underwent so marked a change in magnitude that it may be said to be virtually a re-invention. Where manuscript books even in the best medieval collections were numbered in the hundreds, the books of Renaissance libraries, both printed and manuscript, were cataloged in the thousands. When Rabelais has Gargantua write to Pantagruel, Gargantua says that the world is now full of learned men and "the most extensive libraries" as a direct result of the printing press, which he calls a divinely inspired invention.[11] The growth of libraries in the fifteenth century coincides so closely with the invention of printing and the advancement of humanism that it is impossible to distinguish cause and effect. If humanism fostered book collecting and insured a ready welcome for the printing press, the proliferation of printed books disseminated humanist ide-

ology across Europe and created in humanists a further eagerness to
amass the libraries that enabled their scholarship—and the writing
of new books for the press. Between the middle of the fifteenth
century and the beginning of the seventeenth scores of great libraries
were founded, first in the humanist courts of Italy, then in the
courts and universities of northern Europe. By Burton's lifetime the
revolutionary technology of printing had made possible immense
collections like the Vatican's and, though still in its infancy, the
Bodleian.

The *Anatomy* is impossible to imagine without its author's access
to libraries of this new sort. Indeed, in its attempt to focus the
multiplicity of human knowledge through the single lens of melancholy, the book expresses something of the power of the humanist
library. More than any book one can think of, the *Anatomy* is con-
stituted of books. "Intertextuality" is its very being. Opening the
Anatomy we enter a vast library, an enclosed space where books
convey virtually the only reality; books become the sole means we
have of knowing what lies beyond its walls. Burton, the omnivorous
reader, is librarian and guide to its riches. He appears not only to
have read every shelf but to be its catalog and index. As we read
him, we may be reminded of the personification of memory in *The
Faerie Queene,* the old man "of infinite remembrance" sitting in his
chair surrounded by piles of worm-eaten parchment rolls and manuscript books, "tossing and turning them withouten end" (2:ix, 58).
Like him, Burton seems tied to a never-ending task of searching
and comparing. And through Burton, it appears, we may know all
that the library holds.

But in his case the relative strength of the worker and his tools
is reversed. The old man in Spenser, Eumnestes, or "well remembering," is stocking his memory with frail manuscript documents,
single copies whose existence, even as he reads, is threatened by
"canker holes" and decay. Burton, writing a century and a half into
the age of Gutenberg, need not worry. Hundreds of copies of each
book exist, and a new and more accurate edition may always be
struck off. Happy fact for the scholar, even happier for the writer.
But it also means that the man now no longer has the odds over
his materials; he is subject to them in a new way. Master his books
as he may, once his own words are arrested from the flow of talk,
remanded to writing, and locked in the forms of type, anyone may
check the accuracy of his memory. He is writing not so much to

preserve memory as to rearrange it. Anyone working amid the same books, or in a comparable library, may rearrange them in another way that suits him. Worse yet, even the best of memories may be outdone by the index, another invention that came with the printed book.

One thing Burton never, never does is tell us how he keeps track of the immensity of his material. Has he created a master index for himself from all his reading, a seventeenth-century equivalent of the modern scholar's card file (or better yet, computer diskettes)? Does he depend on the indices printed in the works as well? Were his books arranged in some mnemonic fashion? Neither the *Anatomy* nor his library offers any clue. And, of course, to tell us would break the spell, would breach the decorum which we still share that pretends that every scholar has so internalized his learning that the necessary references come to him effortlessly and without the need to consult notes or index. The ideal here is the learned disputation or conversation, the kind of talk at which Burton was said to have excelled. "No man did surpass him," Anthony à Wood says, "for his ready and dextrous interlarding his common discourses among [the scholars of Christ Church] with Verses from the Poets or Sentences from classical Authors, which being then the fashion in the University, made his Company more acceptable."[12]

As such testimony indicates, Burton was blessed—ambiguously blessed—with a memory of extraordinary power. He quotes from it frequently in the *Anatomy,* especially when he cites favorite classical authors or the Bible. But the very means that enables us to know he is quoting from memory, small variations from the printed texts available to him, point to a reason for melancholy in so learned a man. No matter how retentive his memory, it will never equal the retentiveness of a single printed book. No matter how broad and far-ranging his memory, it will never equal the power of the library in which he sits. In this sense Burton may be understood as a man straddling a culture still oral in many of its habits of thought and perception, in which memory is a significant power of the mind, and the culture of print, in which memory atrophies in response to a technology of codifying information. Wood's phrase "being then the fashion in the University" suggests how far the late seventeenth century had moved from these habits of thought. Pleasure in a memory ready with the apt quotation would—and does—endure, but such ability seems rather decorative than necessary.

"To Be Excellent, To Know All"

But even more significant, and potentially more grievous in the etiology of scholarly melancholy, is the endless proliferation—and relativizing—of authority that printing gives rise to. "What a catalogue of new books all this year, all this age (I say), have our Frankfort marts, our domestic marts brought out," Burton laments. *"Quis tam avidus librorum helluo?* [who is such a hungry glutton of books], who can read them? As already, we shall have a vast chaos and confusions of books, we are oppressed with them, our eyes ache with reading, our fingers with turning" (Democritus to the Reader; 1:24). An individual book may convey knowledge and reassurance. But a multitude of books subverts any hope of arriving at a stable conclusion, a definitive truth. Elizabeth Eisenstein notes how the new libraries stocked with printed books made contradictions in received knowledge more visible, divergent traditions more difficult to reconcile. [13] Printing enabled the building of vast libraries in comparatively short periods of time, especially in the case of the Bodleian, whose founding came when presses had been sending forth books for well over a century. But the process of sorting out the contents of the libraries took considerably longer. Burton, clearly, stands right in the middle of this process. He has several thousand books available to him, on melancholy and, given the inclusiveness of his treatment, on every subject that may relate to it. He discovers, however, that they qualify, contradict, overturn one another to a degree that makes radical uncertainty the only certain outcome of his quest.

Recognition of this is everywhere apparent in his manner of prosecuting his search. His arguments proceed by quotation and appeal to learned authority. But the very method subverts the goal. The more authorities are piled on authorities, the less we feel we know. We realize that this way of arguing could just as easily prove the contrary position. And the contrary position is frequently just where Burton leads us, sometimes with full appreciation of the paradox entailed and sometimes in apparent unconcern that his argument has changed direction. His chapter consoling those whose melancholy comes of being baseborn provides a good example of this. For six pages he cites baseborn men who nevertheless achieved fortune, power, and reputation. Then he appears to catch himself and to fear that he may be misunderstood as casting aspersions on the wellborn.

"Let no *terrae filius,* or upstart, insult at this which I have said, no worthy gentleman take offence" (2.3.2;2:142). He is himself a gentleman, he protests, and does not intend to disparage "true gentry and nobility." True gentility will show itself in gentle conditions, he insists, the common Renaissance answer to anomalies of class and behavior. As this is then developed through examples and citations, it swings around to become the following "If it so fall out (as often it doth) that such peasants are preferred by reason of their wealth, chance, error, etc., or otherwise, yet (as the cat in the fable, when she was turned to a fair maid, would play with mice) a cur will be a cur, a clown will be a clown, he will likely savour of the stock whence he came, and that innate rusticity can hardly be shaken off." We have now come a hundred and eighty degrees from where we began and arrived at another position that may be equally buttressed by learned literary authority. But then his conclusion brings the argument full circle and includes *both* positions: "In a word, many noblemen are an ornament to their order: many poor men's sons are singularly well endowed, most eminent, and well deserving for their worth, wisdom, learning, virtue, valour, integrity; excellent members and pillars of a commonwealth. And therefore, to conclude that which I first intended, to be base by birth, meanly born is no disparagement. *Et sic demonstratur, quod erat demonstrandum*" (2:144). And so also, we may add, has the opposite been proved, and every shade of opinion between them. This is something that threatens everywhere in Burton's manner, the realization that no single opinion is stable or fully trustworthy. There is always another opinion to come, and given the wealth of his memory (which is also his library), contradictory opinions will emerge sooner or later. What we are witnessing is the *copia* of Renaissance humanism becoming skepticism by its own most cherished method.

This diagnosis of the melancholy of late Renaissance humanism, what we might call the melancholy of the printed book, finds support in a recent writer's account of the melancholy inherent in the process of anatomy itself. Describing Vesalius's anatomical illustrations, with their extraordinary sense of the human body suffering under its analytical dismemberment, Devon L. Hodges suggests that there is a paradoxical doubleness about the process: "it is a method for revealing order, but it also causes decay." The anatomist's attempt to uncover a unified truth about his subject "leads him to interrupt that totality and transform it into fragmented matter." The method itself, moreover, "defers and distances the absolute order he hopes to bring to light."[14] In Burton's particular case, the anatomizing of melancholy becomes a process of ordering that is well suited to discovering the disorderly nature of madness, but not to curing it.

Anatomy and melancholy have an affinity; they are both an effect of loss—the loss of meaning, the loss of any clear path to the truth, the loss of power to master an uncertain world. . . . A melancholy sense that something is lost propels a desire to conduct an anatomy—and anatomy itself creates loss. Anatomy, then is a cure for melancholy that creates the conditions that produce it. No wonder then that Burton endlessly writes his *Anatomy of Melancholy*.[15]

To Hodges's sense that Burton's anatomizing uncovers the disorder of madness, I would add that it uncovers as well the disorderly state of what humanity knows, the disorder in the mind of the culture as it confronts its illness. Print was an essential condition of the anatomy he conducted. Printed books enabled Europe to write its knowledge large, and Burton to read it with an unprecedented thoroughness. By means of an anatomy that begins and ends with the printed book, he is led to the melancholy instability of what is known.

Burton is well aware of the tendency to instability and skepticism in his own writing, but there is nothing he is willing to do, or can do, to stop it. The comical zigzagging in "Democritus to the Reader" parodies it self-consciously. When he later poses himself the question what the greatest cause of melancholy may be, his nonanswer expresses this disinclination, or helplessness, to discriminate: "As that gymnosophist in Plutarch made answer to Alexander (demanding which spake best), Every one of his fellows did speak better than the other; so may I say of these causes to him that shall require which is the greatest, every one is more grievous than other, and this of passion the greatest of all" (1.2.3.1;1:250). He both claims that passion is the greatest cause and subverts the claim, but the indecisive decision is overborne by the witty reference to Plutarch that makes light of the whole endeavor of deciding: why should we care to decide such matters, the implication is, while we may use our learning to smile at them. His chapters end typically not with a conclusion or judgment on what has been discussed, but with one last quotation. Another frequent ending is the direction to consult yet another authority—or half a dozen other authorities—for yet more opinions on the subject. Joan Webber calls attention to the frequency with which Burton ends his sentences with *etc.*, "letting the openness of the sentence suggest the infinity that the page cannot contain."[16] A conclusion means closure, but of this the world of learning does not admit. New books constantly enter the library, and every new book must open the case again. For this reason the *Anatomy* could never be conclusively ended during Burton's life. Every three or four years a new edition must add citations to the author's reading since the previous edition. This prescinding from conclusion and generalization comes of Burton's consciousness of the multiplicity of opinion. The only court he appeals to are the books of the learned, where every shade of judgment is to be found. In such a court no final decision can ever be rendered. Burton rarely imposes himself on his authorities. If one authority seems extreme in opinion, he will typically qualify it by reference to another. What counts in the *Anatomy* is the multiplicity of learned opinion, unstable though it is.

This reluctance to generalize or conclude brings to mind another image for Burton's extraordinary power of memory. Jorge Luis Borges' story "Funes the Memorious" tells of an Uruguayan boy of such exact and precisely detailed memory that for him there is virtually no distinction between an event or perception and his recall of it. Funes began with an uncanny sense of time, but after being paralyzed in an accident, finds his power of memory so acute that it leads him to the conviction of the absolute individuality of every object, every perception. Latin, in a happy coincidence with our subject, becomes the link between the narrator and Funes; when the latter borrows the former's books, he is able to learn that most systematic of languages at sight—with no concern for its system. In Borges' formulation, such power of memory is at odds with the power to abstract: Funes is "almost incapable of ideas of a general, Platonic sort." Not only was it difficult for him "to comprehend that the generic symbol *dog* embraces so many unlike individuals of diverse size and form; it bothered him that the dog at three fourteen (seen from the side) could have the same name as the dog at three fifteen (seen from the front)."[17] So acutely able to recall difference, Funes finds abstraction and generalization an assault upon particularity.

Borges' witty sketch sets memory against analysis in a way that
suggests Burton's consciousness of the multiplicity of human judgment on any subject. In the complex of competing opinion the
Anatomy represents, to attempt to resolve such difference, to conclude or to generalize is to offer a kind of violence to the variety of
learned tradition.

Burton does, of course, attempt to analyze his materials in the
synopses of the three partitions of the book. This forms a kind of
exoskeleton, as Ruth Fox has described it, which gives shape to his
progression through the subject of melancholy.[18] But within each
individual member or subsection he is free to remember and to cite
the multitude of opinion that may be brought to bear. The sense
of the multiplicity and the conflict of these opinions is therefore
present at each individual moment in the *Anatomy*. Fox uses the
somewhat anachronistic analogy of the Gothic cathedral to describe
the diversity within unity of the *Anatomy*.[19] But the library offers
the more instructive analogy. Burton's analytic structure in his
synopses is like the external and physical structure for containing
and organizing the knowledge within the library, the rooms, the
cases, the shelves. As the three synopses do with the variety of
learned opinion, the library's catalog groups books by subject matter. But it makes no guarantee of their agreement one with another,
nor does it judge them in their arrangement on the shelves. In
reading the *Anatomy* we browse along shelves arranged by Burton's
memory. The books may be disparate, coming from different areas
of the real library, but Burton has brought them together momen-
tarily in a kind of paratactic order that is not hierarchic or tending
toward judgment. "To be excellent, to know all" we must follow
his lead through the vastness and variety on the subject of melancholy, which is human nature, even though to do so prevents any
final judgments. The library is simply too rich for the search to end
prematurely; it allows us to come to no definitive conclusion.

A Library of a Book

Let us return to the question of definition. We may be tempted
at this point to imitate Burton's own manner and say, with the
gymnosophist in Plutarch, each of the ways the *Anatomy* has been
defined is truer than the others, and whichever one strikes our fancy
is the truest of all. But the analogy of the library may offer a less

desperate alternative. What one makes of the *Anatomy* depends on where in the library one happens to be reading. By turns the book is therapeutic, a sober medical treatise, a general satire on man's folly, a particular satire on individual follies, a consolation, a sermon, an encyclopedia of odd lore, a collection of anecdotes, a collection of proverbs, a religious polemic, a mysogynist tract, a celebration of love. It is serious, amusing, comic, dignified, playful, querulous, religious, skeptical, credulous. One could go on, and in the manner of Rabelais (which is also Burton's) list all the things that the *Anatomy* is. The point would be that the book aims at plenitude, both in its subject matter and in its method. In this it epitomizes the two centuries of Renaissance humanism that aimed at a universality of knowledge. The inclusiveness of the humanist library is the inclusiveness of the *Anatomy*.

In thus describing the book, it should be recognized, we sacrifice to some extent its claims to unity of structure and rhetorical intent. And yet Fox's description of the structure of the *Anatomy*, the best account we have, emphasizes that it is "not a neatly ordered medical, philosophical, and historical exposition of a disease, but a tangled chain which exhibits the order and disorder essential to Burton's explanation of melancholy man." His subject, she suggests, is "not so much man as it is man's knowledge of himself." Hence his structure, with its digressions and excesses, displays "man inquiring into what he knows about himself."[20] Even the ordinary reader recognizes that there is something of a rearguard action against epistemological chaos in Burton's manner of prosecuting his argument. It is as if the richness of what man may know threatens everywhere to overwhelm his powers to contain it. Not that the *Anatomy* is chaotic; we can recognize a kind of order in the seeming perplexity. But we are more likely to be impressed by the copiousness and inclusiveness of the book than by its logic.

In a sense there are two books coexisting in the *Anatomy*, never really separate but at the same time at odds with each other. One is the complete medical treatise on melancholy, an "anatomy" properly speaking. The other is a work of humanist wisdom, a kind of commentary on human nature and, implicitly, on human knowing. This second book finds its ancestor in Erasmus's *Praise of Folly* and its other paradox-obsessed kin. This is the book that begins in Democritus to the Reader and surfaces in the various digressions that enlarge our sense of what we can know of melancholy and of humanity.[21] I say they are at odds because the medical treatise aims to define its subject and express its scope. But the "other" book does not limit or define but includes everything human under the aegis of melancholy. For this reason digression is its mode, a kind of formless form that may strike into any area of human knowing. It may become a general satire, a utopia, a complaint, a consolation, a listing of proverbs, or a sermon. And this is the book that most continues to fascinate us.

We read Burton, it needs to be emphasized, more for his manner than his matter. We never forget that Burton knew nothing of the circulation of the blood, even though Harvey, his almost exact contemporary, published his findings the same year as the third edition of the *Anatomy*, 1628. This Copernican revolution of medicine puts a gulf of understanding between Burton's science and our own. And so it is with much of his other lore. We read the science of the *Anatomy* as historians, interested in it, primarily, for its strangeness, a wholly other way of describing something that we understand differently. Because there is a continuity of culture between ourselves and the early seventeenth century, we recognize the same patterns of mental suffering in the melancholy Burton describes. But we understand many of the etiologies of what we call depression in wholly other ways, especially the physical dimensions. If the book epitomizes Renaissance humanism, it cannot escape being very much of its own time. This is a part of its value to students of the seventeenth century, for it embodies so much of the knowledge and so many of the attitudes and beliefs of the time.

But we remain interested in the *Anatomy* not only as historians because so many of its habits of mind remain recognizably contiguous to our own. We revel in Burton's learning less for its content than for its capacity and readiness, which continue to astonish. Burton has a faith in the printed word that is at once credulous and skeptical, but a faith that keeps him endlessly turning leaves. Books and knowledge are clearly life to him. Implicit in his search is the belief that if one can know all that can be known, the human mind can somehow overcome the ills that beset it. Orthodox Christian that he is, he would (and does) explicitly deny this. But it is the assumption, problematic though it may be, that motivates his search, keeps him adding to his book in each new edition. To him melancholy is a condition that may be overcome by the weight of the combined knowledge of all who have written, wisely or foolishly, about it.

Language, Burton's ceaseless flow of words, becomes the other antidote of melancholy. From his learning comes a seemingly inexhaustible *copia* of language, or a *copia* of two languages, for Burton's prose is, as he calls it, "my *Macaronicon*," moving back and forth between the frequently racy English he addresses to the reader and the Latin origin of his learning. His mind is obviously as stocked with Latin as with English; he thinks in both languages, sometimes at once. And from the conjunction of the two languages emerges an extraordinary copiousness. He illustrates as he admits the "faults" of his style: "And for those other faults of barbarism, Doric dialect, extemporanean style, tautologies, apish imitation, a rhapsody of rags gathered together from several dung-hills, excrements of authors, toys and fopperies confusedly tumbled out, without art, invention, judgment, wit, learning, harsh, raw, rude, phantastical, absurd, insolent, indiscreet, ill-composed, indigested, vain, scurrile, idle, dull, and dry; I confess all ('tis partly affected), thou canst not think worse of me than I do of myself" (Democritus to the Reader; 1:26). Though he confesses to affecting such a style, we somehow believe him when he says he publishes his book "as it was first written, *quicquid in buccam venit* [whatever came to mouth], in an extemporean style, as I do commonly all other exercises, *effudi quicquid dictavit genius meus* [I poured out whatever the mind dictated], out of a confused company of notes, and writ with as small deliberation as I do ordinarily speak, without all affectation of big words, fustian phrases, jingling terms, tropes, strong lines, that like Acestes' arrows caught fire as they flew, strains of wit, brave heats, elogies, hyperbolical exornations, elegancies, etc., which many so much affect" (Democritus to the Reader; 1:31). Living in two languages appears to have given a particular richness to Burton's word hoard. He frequently speaks a thesaurus of words, spinning out a list that moves from the colloquial to the inkhorn. His discourses on a given subject have a similarly inexhaustible quality to them; he can go on for pages of examples, proverbs, quotations, finally interrupting himself but persuading the reader that he could have continued almost indefinitely. The strange result of this near caricature of *copia* is that Burton rarely exhausts but rather nourishes and refreshes the reader. His prose is like a source, a wellhead of language, where learning seems to flow immediately and effortlessly into a stream of words.

So too his book has a similar appeal. One goes to it now not to cure melancholy but to encounter the curious mixture that it is. On the one hand—and this is its primary reality—the *Anatomy* epitomizes the desire of Renaissance humanism to understand human nature by concentration on the knowledge of the past. On the other, it stands at the margin, but only at the margin, of more modern scientific habits of mind. Burton was intensely interested in many of the writers we now credit with the beginnings of experimental science. But he did not recognize their difference, or the difference of their methods, from the other authorities he cites. His own methods are those of traditional humanism, but magnified by the power of the libraries of printed books available to him. A consequence of this are the epistemological problems he inevitably encounters. Hodges suggests that the concern of the anatomy genre with such problems "reveals it as a transitional form, a form uncertain about its relation to an older discourse of patterning or to the new analytical discourse of science it helps bring into being."[22] Unlike other anatomists, Burton's stronger allegiance is to the earlier discourse. Three and a half centuries later we have grown more used to the epistemological problems he encountered, the instability and relativity of human knowledge. But one of the fascinations of the *Anatomy* is seeing Burton's intermittent and partial awareness of them. The discourse of the *Anatomy* stands at one of those crossing points of mental history, between habits of mind we know as ours and those we recognize only from the past. And even as we recognize the problems raised by his method, we constantly acknowledge the immensity of his learning, the readiness of his memory.

Chapter Three
A World of Melancholy

The *Anatomy of Melancholy* is the rich and complex book it is because of the way Burton transformed his subject. He began with one sense of melancholy, but under his hand it grew into something much larger to become indeed a means of viewing all of human life. In the early seventeenth century melancholy was a quite specific form of mental suffering, an identifiable disease that corresponds to what we would call depression. As such it was described as being physically located in particular parts of the human body and caused— or at least aggravated—by diet, physical constitution, air, aging, and other material causes. This is the melancholy that may be anatomized in the physical sense. Early in "Democritus to the Reader" Burton tells of Hippocrates' being summoned by the people of Abdera to examine Democritus, whom they suspected of madness because of his continual laughter. Hippocrates found Democritus engaged in cutting up various beasts to find the cause of melancholy and madness, but pronounced him sane after hearing the soundness of his moral anatomy of the world. We never learn what the physician thinks of the philosopher's literal anatomizing of the animals. But in terms of the late Renaissance understanding of melancholy, there is nothing strange on the face of it about the supposition that the disease may be discovered, like a tumor or diseased organ, within the body itself.

Melancholy as a Disease

This sense of melancholy as a physical disease derived from the humoral theory attributed to Hippocrates and refined by Galen in the second century A.D. According to the theory, proper physical health, as well as a balanced personality, requires a tempering of the four humors, blood, phlegm, yellow bile, and black bile. The predominance of black bile, melancholia, over the other three causes a depressed state of mind and dangerously weakens one's overall health. Such is the general theory which in the millenium and a half after Galen would undergo various additions and elaborations. One significant elaboration was the connection of the humors with planetary influences by ninth-century Arabic astrological writers, the sanguine with Jupiter, the phlegmatic with the moon, choler (yellow bile) with Mars, and melancholy with Saturn.[1] In the early Renaissance Marsilio Ficino and his Neoplatonic followers revised the tradition of melancholy as a baleful, diseased state and posited a heroic melancholy as the basis of genius. Drawing inspiration from the pseudoAristotelian Problem XXX, they asserted that the melancholy temperament was the basis of all accomplishment in philosophy, poetry, politics, and the arts. Though the melancholy humor in excess could lead to the diseased state of depression and despondency, in moderate predominance it excited the superiority of genius.[2] This reinterpretation gave rise to a fashion of melancholy in the sixteenth century, one that Shakespeare mocks in Jaques in *As You Like It.* Burton occasionally sports with this sense of melancholy—and refers to "that old aphorism of Aristotle . . . *Nullum magnum ingenium sine mixtura dementiae*" (1.3.3;1:422). But it remained the minority view, and by the end of the century the understanding of melancholy as a specific and debilitating form of mental suffering clearly dominated other thinking. Melancholy was acknowledged to be a serious illness, and when afflicted by it, one sought medical treatment.[3]

This is the perspective on melancholy with which Burton began writing the *Anatomy,* and once we enter the treatise proper, it dominates the first section. In 1.1.1.3 he defines melancholy in relation to other diseases of the head, frenzy, madness, and dotage, and in subsection 5 distinguishes this proper melancholy from the transitory "melancholy dispositions" which everyone suffers from time to time. In member 2 there follow nine subsections that form a "digression of anatomy," in which the body, soul, and faculties are described. This becomes a necessary prelude to the physical description of the disease. It is named from its material cause of melancholia (1.1.3.1). This melancholy humor offends in either quantity or quality, affecting the overall humoral balance of the body, most frequently by its cold and dry temperature. (Various authorities also believed that certain compound sorts of melancholy arose from "adust" or burnt states of the other humors.) In orthodox fashion Burton then divides melancholy into three kinds according to which part of the body is affected by the melancholy humor:

head melancholy, "from the sole fault of the brain"; melancholy of the whole body, "when the whole temperature is melancholy"; and lastly hypochondriacal or windy melancholy, which centers on the bowels, liver, spleen, or mesentery.

For the first forty-odd pages of the treatise proper Burton treats melancholy as a physical condition, describing and locating it as a specific disease, or rather a series of related diseases. Then, as he begins to consider the causes of melancholy in section 2, we are startled by the title of his first subsection, "God a Cause." The whole tenor of the book changes as Burton canvasses, from Scriptural testimony, ancient history, saints' legends and anecdotes, the ways in which God may send mental affliction as a punishment for sin. Melancholy is not distinguished from but now conflated with madness and other aberrant behavior. Following this a rich "Digression of the Nature of Spirits" (1.2.1.2) takes the reader further into the odd lore of demons, nature spirits, ghosts, and fairies. We have by now strayed a long way from the medical textbook. But it is for sections such as this that we read the *Anatomy*, when Burton's passion for the strange and marvelous takes hold and plunges us into the beliefs and half-beliefs of the seventeenth century.

Melancholy as the Human Condition

In such sections of the *Anatomy* there emerges another sense of melancholy. It becomes not so much a specific disease, let alone one that may be physically isolated, but rather the very condition and ground of human life. This melancholy scarcely admits definition. It can only be described and expatiated on through every facet of mortality. This is the sense of melancholy that predominates in "Democritus to the Reader," the 120-page preface Burton added in the second edition which pretends to introduce the book but which in its manner becomes something of an epitome of the whole. Here melancholy is not to be distinguished from other forms of mental suffering. Indeed in the context one may sense something excessively literal-minded, even comic, in Democritus's anatomizing the carcasses of animals to find the seat of melancholy. Burton proposes "to make a brief survey of the world" in which "thou shalt soon perceive that all the world is mad, that it is melancholy, dotes; that it is . . . made like a fool's head (with that motto, *Caput helloboro dignum*); a crazed head, *cavea stultorum*, a fools' paradise, or

as Apollonius, a common prison of gulls, cheaters, flatters, etc.,
and needs to be reformed" (1:39). The "brief survey" (some sixty
pages!) enforces the idea that melancholy in this sense is general,
that even the wisest philosophers suffered from it. "In this sense we
are all fools," he insists, "we and our writings are shallow and
imperfect . . . even in our ordinary dealings we are no better than
fools" (1:45).

In "Democritus to the Reader," which Burton most likely added
after the *Anatomy* was substantially completed, melancholy is transformed from a specific disease to human folly; the general satire of
Erasmus's *Praise of Folly* becomes the closest analogue of Democritus's satire. Because folly is a moral state rather than a physical one,
this melancholy includes all professions and human institutions,
"kingdoms, provinces, and politic bodies." Countries as well as
individuals may be melancholy, and Burton convicts England of the
malady in its various infirmities, its comparatively uncultivated
state, its many "rogues and beggars, thieves, drunkards, and discontented persons," its lack of attractive cities and its neglect of
trade, for example. He writes not so much an attack or satire on
England as a catalog of its ills in comparison with the rest of Europe.
If all the world is melancholy, then so is England, and these are its
particular symptoms. As a cure for this melancholy, and as the
logical conclusion of the design of reform he postulated in his diagnosis of universal madness, Burton creates his own version of
another humanist genre, the utopia. It differs from More's in being
self-avowedly personal, made "to satisfy and please myself . . . a
poetical commonwealth of mine own" (1:97). It becomes more a
collection of reformist ideas than the imaginatively created place of
the original *Utopia*. Burton appears interested rather in showing the
extent of man's folly and the multiple ways it may be corrected.

In the concluding pages of the preface he admits that he has given
melancholy a second sense, that the preceding discussion has been
of those who are "improperly melancholy, or metaphorically mad"
(1:120). He has not been using melancholy in a medical but rather
in a figurative sense. In the discourse which follows he will "anatomize this humour of melancholy, through all his parts and species,
as it is an habit, or an ordinary disease, and that philosophically,
medicinally, to show the causes, symptoms, and several cures of it,
that it may be the better avoided." But Burton cannot keep to the
medical sense of melancholy, and in fact the whole of the *Anatomy*

oscillates between melancholy as a disease and melancholy as a metaphor or, more properly, melancholy as a metonymy of human misery. Though the syntax does not reflect this, it is as if "philosophically" and "medicinally" represent not synonymous but opposing categories.

As we turn the page and begin reading the first partition, we find ourselves not yet in the promised medical book but in an oration on the dignity, and indignity, of man. "Man, the most excellent and noble creature of the world," Burton begins in good humanist fashion, and goes on to wrap man in a paragraph of praise as the microcosm and model of the world. Then he plunges him into the misery of his fall. Our literal, medical melancholy is just one of the miseries that beset man in his fallen state, but this metonymic melancholy can be seen as very nearly identical with that fallen state. "And last of all," he concludes his list of man's debilities, "that which crucifies us most, is our own folly, madness (*quos Jupiter perdit dementat*; by subtraction of His assisting grace God permits it), weakness, want of government, our facility and proneness in yielding to several lusts, in giving way to every passion and perturbation of the mind: by which means we metamorphose ourselves and degenerate into beasts" (1.1.1.1;1:136). This madness appears not an addition to the list, but is the moral state that sums them all up, the melancholy Democritus Junior had described in the satirical preface and that Old Democritus had vainly sought in his literal anatomy of animals. When he comes to summarize the symptoms of melancholy, Burton insists on the impossibility of any scientific taxonomy. "The four-and-twenty letters make no more variety of words in divers languages than melancholy conceits produce diversity of symptoms in several persons" (1.3.1.4;1:408). The variety of human nature is the variety of melancholy. The disease is protean in the way it shifts shapes, insinuates itself into the symptoms of other diseases. The lesson Burton draws from this is that "the best and soundest of us all is in great danger," that we should recognize our fragility, "remember our miseries and vanities, examine and humiliate ourselves, seek to God, and call to Him for mercy." Melancholy is always at hand, something anyone may slip into, both reminder and scourge of human sinfulness.

The uncertain etiology of melancholy is what enables Burton to make it a metonymy for the fallen human condition. Although melancholy is a disease with specific physical dimensions, he comes to no final decision about whether the spirit and its tribulations cause the bodily suffering or the reverse: "For as the distraction of the mind, amongst other outward causes and perturbations, alters the temperature of the body, so the distraction and distemper of the body will cause a distemperature of the soul, and 'tis hard to decide which of these two do more harm to the other" (1.2.5.1;1:374). Plato lays the fault on the soul, and Galen on the body, each authority claiming for his own special province the lion's share of the blame. And for all that our medicine has advanced beyond Burton's, no satisfactory resolution of this conundrum has yet been found. From this radical uncertainty comes his understanding of melancholy as *the* expression of man's fallen state. For both body and soul were affected by the Fall, the humors of the body becoming distempered and concupiscent and the soul deriving its tendency to selfishness and evil.

This second melancholy, melancholy as metonymy for the human condition, accounts for the way the *Anatomy* aims at universality. As the book grew through successive editions, this metonymic melancholy became its real subject and melancholy as a disease merely a subspecies of it. Lawrence Babb notes how Burton added much more generously to the nontechnical sections of the *Anatomy* than to those concerned with medicine and psychology.[4] The structure of the book—and our experience of it—confirm this development; as we read, we notice that the physical dimensions of melancholy recede, and its emblematic nature grows steadily more prominent. This sense of melancholy as a general state meant that the digressions became essential not only to the method but also to the subject. The real energy of the *Anatomy*, in fact, goes into the great nonmedical sections of the book.[5] Readers are less likely to be struck by the medical sections than by "Democritus to the Reader," the "Digression of Spirits," "Love of Learning, or overmuch Study" (1.2.3.15), the "Digression of the Air" (2.2.3), "Exercise Rectified of Mind and Body" (2.2.4), the moral essays of part 2 which arm the mind against the various discontents of life, and the treatments of love melancholy and religious melancholy in part 3. This comes not only of our lesser interest in the lore of an outdated medicine. Burton himself tips the balance. David Renaker's analysis of the apparently Ramist method of the *Anatomy* calls attention to the fact that the general causes of melancholy take up 232 pages—and the great majority of these on what we would identify as moral rather than physical causes—while a page and a half suffice for the particular causes of head melancholy. Burton "licentiously expands the topics that interest him and hurries through the ones that do not with unmistakable impatience."[6] Though he means the book as a serious treatment of medical melancholy, the divine, and more particularly the humanist, in him take precedence over the physician in the dominance of melancholy as metonymic of humanity's fallen state.

We see this reflected as well in the scholarship that Burton brings to bear on melancholy. It has been estimated that he refers to some 1250 authors, not including biblical writers, in the course of the *Anatomy*. Fewer than two hundred of these are medical authorities.[7] The book he quotes most frequently is the Bible—over six hundred times, an average of once every other page. Galen, the most important medical authority of antiquity, he cites eighty times. But Virgil enters the *Anatomy* just as frequently. Burton quotes Horace, his apparent favorite among the Roman poets, 170 times, and Ovid 130. Both Plato and St. Augustine are cited far more often than any medical writer. Burton obviously knows the medical literature well, but it represents a fraction of the learning he displays in the *Anatomy*. Behind this melancholy lies not the authority of a single field of human knowledge, but in primary position the literature of antiquity, and in the center of this the Bible. After the Bible, Seneca, "divine Seneca," probably stands highest with him among the moral writers of Latin antiquity. "When I read Seneca," he says, " 'methinks I am beyond all human fortunes, on the top of a hill above mortality.' " (2.2.4;2:94).[8] The whole corpus of literature inherited from antiquity, poetry, philosophy, theology, history, natural science, augmented in particular by the literature of the previous two centuries, stands behind his conception of melancholy. Medicine is a substantial part of this last category, but he is just as interested in contemporary books of cosmography, travel, and exploration. Among the Renaissance writers with whom Burton appears to feel the most affinity are neither the medical authorities nor the divines, but the great polymaths of the age, Conrad Gesner, the Scaligers, and especially Jerome Cardan.[9]

Burton's learning in fact is crucial to the way he generalizes melancholy into the ground of human life. He was not formed as a physician, but as a divine. His fundamental training therefore was dialectical and rhetorical. This fact stands behind his tendency to make the most of whatever topic is before him. He is not in a primary way analyzing it as part of a larger whole, but arguing for and persuading his reader of its crucial significance. Because of his rhetorical training, he brings the weight of his learning to bear on every subject. Any particular cause, symptom, or cure of melancholy attains an almost independent importance as we are reading, especially as support for it may come from a variety of fields of knowledge.[10] Whatever frustration this may cause the actual melancholiac who is weighing the elements of cause and cure, it enriches the individual discussion. The degree of enrichment may indeed become quite disproportionate if the topic has worked its way with Burton's imagination. Humanist *copia* urges him toward expansion and elaboration, and under its influence melancholy expands far beyond its recognized medical boundaries.

Burton's Moral Psychology

What it expands into, primarily, is a moral thing. If the relative length of the discussions is any indication, Burton appears to grow skeptical about the physical, material dimensions of melancholy. Only a fifth of section 2, for example, is devoted to physical cures. He goes dutifully through such remedies as diet, evacuation, physic of various kinds, surgery, cordials, and so forth. But these chapters tend to become lists, and our doubt about the efficacy of such remedies grows in direct proportion to the length of the list. He frequently allows the discussion of various forms of physic to grow circular, as he does, for example, with tobacco considered as purgative simple:

Tobacco, divine, rare, superexcellent tobacco, which goes far beyond all the panaceas, potable gold, and philosophers' stones, a sovereign remedy to all diseases. A good vomit, I confess, a virtuous herb, if it be well qualified, opportunely taken, and medicinally used; but as it is commonly abused by most men, which take it as tinkers do ale, 'tis a plague, a mischief, a violent purger of goods, lands, health; hellish, devilish, and damned tobacco, the ruin and overthrow of body and soul. (2.4.2.1;2:228)

As the rhetoric performs an about-face, the herb that may be restorative in physic becomes malevolent in its moral misuse.

On the question of diet Burton allows common sense to subvert entirely the basic understanding of humoral medicine. He concludes two chapters on "diet rectified" in quality and quantity by advising, "when all is said pro and con, Cardan's rule is best, to keep that we are accustomed unto, though it be naught" (2.2.1.2;2:28–29). We should, moreover, follow our own disposition, even to the point of sometimes eating a harmful dish "if we have an extraordinary liking to it." Experience is the best physician: "let every man observe, and be a law unto himself." Good advice, no doubt, but humoral theory held that various foods were transformed directly into particular humors, that one could control the composition of these humors by attention to diet. The only rule of diet Burton finally recognizes is moderation—again simple common sense. A similar skepticism enters the discussion of physic when he takes note of the way fashion rules what doctors prescribe: "*Quisque suum placitum quo capiatur habet:* every man as he likes; so many men so many minds" (2.4.1.5;2:223).

The real energy of Burton's literary therapy goes into essays advocating moral recognition and control. Because of his tendency to develop each point rhetorically, one needs to be cautious of his individual judgments. Still, his insistence on the primacy of rightly ordering the mind and its passions bears conviction: "Whosoever he is that shall hope to cure this malady in himself or any other," he begins, "must first rectify these passions and perturbations of the mind; the chiefest cure consists in them" (2.2.6.1;2:102). The conviction comes in the prominence of this theme in part 2: over a hundred of the 260 pages are devoted to a series of twelve moral essays, 2.2.6.1 to 2.3.8, on gaining control of one's own mental powers and in fortifying the mind with arguments against the discontents of life. Plato had believed that the body's sufferings proceeded from the soul, and even Galen, "the common master" of all who treat the body, had boasted of curing some "by the right settling alone of their minds" (2.2.6.1;2:103). In the second of these therapeutic persuasions Burton expresses his belief in the priority of mental over corporeal treatment: "If he desire aught, let him be satisfied; if in suspense, fear, suspicion, let him be secured: and if it may conveniently be, give him his heart's content; for the body cannot be cured till the mind be satisfied" (2.2.6.2;2:112). It is not impossible that Burton may elsewhere express the reverse opinion, but the proportions of the *Anatomy* suggest that this is his judgment of the order to be followed in curing psychosomatic illness.

Burton recognizes the terrible grip that melancholy may have over its sufferers. His usual way of admitting this fact is to allow the melancholiac to speak, to argue his case rhetorically in his prose. But he refuses to yield to the helplessness or determinism that such arguments imply. For him melancholy remains finally a moral state and as such subject to all the moral defenses that human beings must employ.[11] The cure must begin with the patient himself; he must strive as best he can not to cherish "those fond imaginations which so covertly creep into his mind." The imagination is the faculty subject to melancholy, so the cure must begin with the will. The melancholiac "may choose whether he will give way too far unto it, he may in some sort correct himself" (2.2.6.1;2:106). But if judgment be so impaired, reason and will so weakened, that the sufferer cannot help himself, Burton recommends sharing the misery with a friend. What is lacking in his own reason and will the friend will supply.

The therapeutic medium, of course, is language. Here we see the essentially humanistic character of Burton's melancholy. Though the body may be treated in various ways, with diet, physic, surgical remedies, the principal therapy comes through words. On this both Scripture and gentile learning agree. "Heaviness of the heart of man doth bring it down, but a good word rejoiceth it," he quotes from Proverbs 12:25. *"Oratio namque saucii animi est remedium,"* Plutarch affirms, "a gentle speech is the true cure of a wounded soul" (2.2.6.2;2:112). What Burton makes explicit here in the counsel a friend may offer the melancholiac is implicit throughout the *Anatomy*. Language is the truest antidote, the best physic to melancholy. Talk, whether counsel drawn from the ancients or ramblings among contemporary pharmacopia, has an efficacy in itself for one tempted by solitary silence and self-absorption. I want to suggest in the next chapter that this has important implications for Burton's style in the *Anatomy*. But it also explains his method against melancholy considered as the type of human misery. A digression can never be impertinent if it holds the reader's attention, speaks to him of things that draw him from his solipsism. In the "Consolatory Digression" that follows several pages later he says that because he has made much "of good counsel, comfortable speeches, persuasion, how necessarily they are required to the cure of a discontented or troubled mind," he has thought it well to collect together some of the consolations of the best orators, philosophers, divines, and fathers of the Church (2.3.1.1;2:126). This, of course, is no different from what he always does, weaving together his discourse from quotations and references to ancient and modern learning.[12] Now he admits he cannot even be confident that it will do any good: "'Tis to no purpose in that vulgar phrase to use a company of obsolete sentences and familiar sayings," for the melancholy are too afflicted to attend, and the fortunate have no need of consolation. By calling attention both to what he is doing and to its doubtful efficacy, he makes the reader aware that he is always enwrapping him in the speech of many centuries. *"Non meus hic sermo* [and literally it is not, for he quotes Horace!], 'tis not my speech this, but of Seneca, Plutarch, Epictetus, Austin, Bernard, Christ and His Apostles. . . . If it be not for thy ease, it may be for mine own." Doubtless he intends us to hear an ironic "only" here; 'tis *only* the speech of the wisest men who have ever spoken. Burton's speech puts us in contact with their speech. While we read him we are part of a conversation extending from this particular moment to the point where written speech began. If the reader's mind cannot be touched by something within this whole extent of human community, if he is so deaf to the consolation of language, what hope can there be for him?

This may also explain why Latin is so important to Burton's manner. He differs from other humanists in according Greek no special prestige. He generally quotes Greek authors in Latin, and in the *Anatomy* Homer and Plato as well as Virgil and Seneca speak to us in Latin. Bible verses, too, frequently appear in Latin. Because he lives his scholarly life in Latin, it is for him the language that ties the individual to the larger conversation that extends over time and over national and religious boundaries. The language becomes a kind of bridge from the present to the ancient cultures and acquires in the process something of the status of a universal tongue. For Burton Latin seems at times to have the incantatory power he attributes to good speech itself, " 'Tis *incantionis instar,* a charm, *aestuantis animi refrigerium"* [cooling comfort for the parched spirit] (2.2.6.2;2:112). Latin represents for him human communication in its most universal form, and perhaps for this reason he uses it as almost a talisman in his English prose.

The Therapy of Knowledge

If language brings the consolation of companionship to the melancholy spirit, it also offers the possibility of diversion from the sole concentration on self. Two sections of part 2 emphasize this in

particular. The first of these is one of the great set pieces of the
Anatomy, "Air rectified, with a digression of the Air" (2.2.3). Actually the "Digression of Air" comes first, and while reading it we
are left in a state of uncertainty about what it all has to do with
finding the proper climate for the melancholy sufferer, a topic which
emerges only in the final few pages. But it is evident from his
splendid opening sentence that "air," like melancholy, has been
given a metaphoric cast, that it will come to mean something more
than the element man breathes:

As a long-winged hawk, when he is first whistled off the fist, mounts
aloft, and for his pleasure fetcheth many a circuit in the air, still soaring
higher and higher till he be come to his full pitch, and in the end when
the game is sprung, comes down amain, and stoops upon a sudden: so
will I, having now come at last into these ample fields of air, wherein I
may freely expatiate and exercise myself for my recreation, awhile rove,
wander round about the world, mount aloft to those ethereal orbs and
celestial spheres, and so descend to my former elements again. (2.2.3;2:34–
35)

"These ample fields of air," at first somewhat puzzling to the reader,
comes in the course of the digression to mean the vast resources of
human knowledge, and Burton's freedom is a freedom from his topic
of melancholy. In fact, we hear nothing of melancholy for twenty-
five pages, until he abruptly announces that "my melancholy spaniel's quest, my game, is sprung, and I must suddenly come down
and follow" (2:61). Only then does he return to the question of
health and the nature of literal air. But he leaves the connecting
terms of his metaphor unstated and somewhat mysterious. What
do the ample fields of knowledge have to do with the air we breathe?
The reader, exhilarated by the scope of Burton's meditations, is left
to puzzle it out.

As he tells us in "Democritus to the Reader," Burton "never
travelled but in map or card, in which my unconfined thoughts
have freely expatiated, as having ever been especially delighted with
the study of cosmography" (1:18). Compared to this means of travel,
he seems to imply, any other would be confining. In the "Digression
of Air" he makes good this claim. His travel has been entirely
within the realm of words, and yet he has gone much farther than
any literal voyager could possibly go. The real point, however, is
not the claim of knowledge. There seems scarcely an indicative mood

in the essay; the weight falls rather on the conditional, the subjunctive: " 'Tis fit to be inquired whether . . ." "I would see . . ." "I would examine . . ." "I would find out . . ." As Fox notes, "Burton basks in the multiplicity of 'whethers' as he progresses from theory to theory."[13] The emphasis falls on what *may* be known, what *could* be inquired into. Certainty of knowledge exists just beyond our grasp in the digression, but the result of such skepticism here is not melancholy but exhilaration.

Burton seems to survey the world he knows, but in fact is surveying human knowledge of it. The result is dizzying, intoxicating in its sense of possibility. The reader is positioned between what is known and what might be known about the world, and in the questions the whole extent of seventeenth-century knowledge of the natural world seems to pass in review before him. It seems entirely appropriate that Burton's first inquiry concerns the variation of the compass and the explanations of why the magnetic needle points north. For this leads him, just as it had led Europe, into an exploration of the face of the globe and the terrae incognitae, both literal and figurative, that still await discovery. He "would censure" all the lies in the writings of travelers and natural historians, "correct those errors in navigation, reform cosmographical charts, and rectify longitudes" (2.2.3;2:40). Then he descends under the surface of the earth to speculate about geology and infernal realms. There is throughout a wonderful hybridization of scientific information and methods grafted onto ancient assumptions, as in the controversy he reports between Franciscus Ribera, who calculates the dimensions of hell as two hundred Italian miles in diameter, and Lessius, who believes it "one Dutch mile in diameter, all filled with fire and brimstone; because, as he there demonstrates, that space, cubically multiplied, will make a sphere able to hold 800,000 millions of damned bodies (allowing each body six foot square)," and the damned are unlikely to exceed 100,000 million (2:42). When the inquiry reascends to the surface, it takes up questions of climate and its effects on the temperaments of populations. Then meteorology ascends further into astronomy. In the latter one is frequently reminded of the cosmological discussion between Adam and Raphael in *Paradise Lost*; though Milton was himself an adept in astronomy, the language is sometimes close enough to suggest that he may have used Burton as a compendium. Burton, like Raphael, does not commit himself, but the weight of opinion, as in *Paradise Lost,* appears to be solidly on the side of heliocentrism. [14] He remains open as well to more daring speculation about infinite worlds: "If our world be small in respect, why may we not suppose a plurality of worlds, those infinite stars visible in the firmament to be so many suns, with particular fixed centres; to have likewise their subordinate planets, as the sun hath his dancing still round him?" (2:54–55). But in the final portion of the digression the tone turns satiric as he reports speculations about the nature of God; here, clearly, is a line that human knowledge crosses only at its peril, to fall into absurdity, "the froth of human wit and excrement of curiosity" (2:60). In the larger structure of the *Anatomy* we can notice that this kind of speculation, beyond the legitimate bounds of human knowledge, does not cure but causes the religious melancholy considered in part 3.

When the digression ends and Burton turns to the question proper of how healthful air may benefit the melancholy temperament, we are left with the analogy implied but never concluded that the "air" into which we have been taken for an exhilarating intellectual spin may have just such a beneficial effect. The "air," of course, is the knowledge of the cosmos that Burton has acquired—and imparted—without having left Oxford, without indeed having to leave the Bodleian Library. Language has been the sole means of his voyaging, the only instrument for peering into the heavens. It provides a communal power of knowing far surpassing the resources of the most audacious individual. Burton quotes Seneca to the effect that many people see only the appearance of the heavens, that one age does not suffice for true understanding, but that the labors of succeeding ages will reveal things that are still not understood (2.2.3;2:60). And from J. C. Scaliger he adds an even more suggestive idea "Nequaquam nos homines sumus, sed partes hominis; ex omnibus aliquid fieri potest, idque non magnum; ex singulis fere nihil" (we are not human beings at all, but only parts of a single human; from all of us something can come, and that not great; from the individual, scarcely anything). Or perhaps from the individual comes only melancholy, a kind of nothing, the privation of human feeling? Through language, on the other hand, comes a process of knowing all the more attractive in never being completed but always leaning toward futurity. Not for nothing does the word *melancholy* disappear during the "Digression of Air." There is no time or space for it.

The idea becomes explicit in the following member, "Exercise Rectified" (2.2.4). Melancholy resides in stasis, "too much solitariness and idleness," and the motions of the cosmos, the heavens, the air, the waters, "teach us that we should ever be in action" (2:69). Among all the exercises of body and mind, "there is none so general, so aptly applied to all sorts of men, so fit and proper to expel idleness and melancholy, as that of study" (2:86). Study is any exercise of the mind, and Burton includes the viewing of paintings and sculpture, "old coins of several sorts . . . old relics, Roman antiquities," the curiosities collected from China and the New World. But his own experience of these things has been primarily through books, and on books he centers his recommendation of a breathtaking range of mental occupation:

For what a world of books offers itself, in all subjects, arts, and sciences, to the sweet content and capacity of the reader! In arithmetic, geometry, perspective, optics, astronomy, architecture, *sculptura, pictura,* of which so many and such elaborate treatises are of late written; in mechanics and other mysteries, military matters, navigation, riding of horses, fencing, swimming, gardening, planting, great tomes of husbandry, cookery, falconry, hunting, fishing, fowling, etc., with exquisite pictures of all sports, games, and what not? In music, metaphysics, natural and moral philosophy, philology, in policy, heraldry, genealogy, chronology, etc., they afford great tomes; or those studies of antiquity, etc. (2.2.4;2:88)

Books here recapitulate all the physical exercises recommended earlier in the chapter. At the same time his *et ceteras* give the list an openness to the whole range of mental experience. In the twelve pages that follow he expatiates on the possibilities of study, providing in effect an annotated bibliography for any literate melancholiac. When read against the background of the preceding "Digression of Air," Burton's meaning becomes clear enough: the stolid self-absorption of melancholy is most effectively countered in being directed outward to the mysteries of the natural world and the breadth of human experience enfolded in books. This is, of course, the understanding encoded in the very method of the *Anatomy*. The constant reference outward to the sources of human knowledge pulls the reader away from sole concentration on the self. The true therapy of humanism, the therapy of language, rests in this implicit counsel to read and to know.

The Third Partition

In the final partition Burton very nearly abandons all pretence of writing an orderly account of a medical phenomenon. His subject is love, which he contends is "a species of melancholy, and a necessary part of this my treatise" (3.1.1.1;3:4). But it is at least as apparent that he is taking a final digressive turn from melancholy, that the subject itself pleases him, and that he develops it with only intermittent concern for its relation to melancholy. Insofar as love is a cause of melancholy, we would have expected it logically to be treated in partition 1, section 2, member 3, where the other passionate causes are taken up. But Fox speaks of the structure of the *Anatomy* growing "not vaguely illogical, but definitely so" in the third partition.[15] Whereas the first partition had concerned the causes, symptoms, and prognostics of melancholy and the second the cure of melancholy, now causes, symptoms, and cures are each treated successively in each of the three sections of the partition. Even the division of love melancholy itself seems illogical. The first two sections are related in that they treat "heroical melancholy," or passionate love, then jealousy, which is love turned to mistrust and hatred. But the final section concerns religious melancholy, which is related only in deriving from love of God. In the third partition, as Fox notes, Burton seems careless or unconcerned with the categories that organize his discourse; "species" can be made synonymous with "symptoms," and the rules of art rather than logic appear to govern it.[16] He as much as gives up any pretence of order and logic as he admits the frankly recreative character of his final partition: "after a harsh and unpleasing discourse of melancholy, which hath hitherto molested your patience and tired the author, give him leave with Godefridus the lawyer, and Laurentius (cap. 5), to recreate himself in this kind after his laborious studies" (3.1.1.1;3:6). He claims the liberty of other grave and learned scholars "to refresh my Muse a little" and "to season a surly discourse with a more pleasing aspersion of love matters."

There seems indeed an added licentiousness to Burton's method in the final part. Melancholy disappears from view for pages at a time, and love becomes a subject in itself with only occasional reference to the way it induces melancholy. After twelve pages of discourse on the way beauty causes love, he admits that "no man doubts of these matters" (3.2.2.2;3:76), then goes on for another twelve pages to enumerate the beautiful features that cause love! Except for the fact that love often makes people unhappy, we wonder what precisely love has to do with melancholy, what justifies its separate treatment in over a third of the total book. The "evidence" Burton cites now makes no pretence of reference to the actual world; poetry and fiction become as important as historical testimony. The gods and goddesses of mythology are as relevant to the argument as passionate mortals, such things "which are to be believed with a poetical faith" (3.2.2.2;3:73). Indeed, it makes no difference where the support for his arguments comes from, since nearly all that he says of love are things that a reader will already know and believe. The interest shifts decisively from the subject to the variety of incident and anecdote.

We might suspect that Burton wishes to generalize his subject even further. If melancholy-as-folly, melancholy as metonymic of the human condition, generalizes the melancholy that is a specific disease, love-as-melancholy raises the generalization to the next higher power. Or perhaps we can say that love is the more general subject because it contains within it the means of overcoming melancholy; if love contains the potential for melancholy, it is also potentially curative. But there is no use pretending that he has some idea about love that he wishes to develop. The real point, for Burton's particular purposes as a writer, is that love is a broader and more generous subject. The very chapter titles and the proportions of his discourse make this evident. "Other causes of Love-Melancholy, Sight, Beauty from the face, eyes, and other parts, and how it pierceth" (3.2.2.2) takes twenty-three pages to express the startling idea that beauty frequently causes people to fall in love. The next subsection, "Artificial Allurements of Love," spends even longer, thirty-eight pages, informing us that art is a powerful supplement to nature in this same circumstance. "Symptoms or Signs of Love-Melancholy, in Body, Mind, good, bad, etc." (3.2.3) suggests that lovers frequently grow pale, blush, sigh, cannot sleep, that they embrace, kiss, look into each other's eyes, experience uncertainty in their moods, act silly, and are unreasonably devoted to each other. The whole of this second section, almost two hundred pages, leads to the advice that "The last and best Cure of Love-Melancholy is, to let them have their Desire" (3.2.5.5), that lovers had best marry. There needs no Burton come from the library to tell us this, we reasonably object. But a reasonable objection has little force in the flow of imagination

Burton taps in these chapters. As reasonably object that an anthology of love poems has only one subject.

The best analogue of this treatment of love melancholy and jealousy is the "Digression of Air." As Burton leads the reader there through what is known of the world, here he leads one through the stores of the poetic imagination. Love is at the center of his discourse, we may suspect, as much because it has been the mainspring of the human imagination as because it causes melancholy. "Beauty a Cause" pretends to inform us of this fact but in fact delights us with the variety of ways this is illustrated in works of the imagination. It becomes in fact a kind of prose blazon in which scores of mistresses are celebrated by scores of poets, in which the multiplication of illustration is not a vice but a virtue. And just as the blazon is a catalog, so are these chapters catalogs of the ways the common experience of love has been expressed in the culture. Burton's prose collects, anthologizes, makes a collage of the best and oddest bits from the storehouse of literary experience. In section 2, on jealousy, his discourse becomes almost anthropological as he details the ways in which the dark side of love has been dealt with in various cultures. The real objection might well be not that we already know what is being described, but that we miss something that might well have been included. For example, when he catalogs the instances that show black eyes as the "most amiable, enticing and fairest," we miss a reference to Shakespeare's sonnets (which Burton seems not to know). The aim, in short, is not to express an idea efficiently but to delight the reader with the extent of literature's recognition of the common facts of love. By turns he pleases us with references we already know and surprises us with ones we have never heard. The essays on love melancholy are tours de force of collection, and their aim is to impress us with the variety and vagaries of love as well as of the imagination which has played over it. In terms of tone they extend from his sermon on charity at the beginning of the partition to the comedy of the final essay on jealousy, in which self-gelding and marrying whores are both recounted as means some have taken to cure jealousy.

In the final section of partition 3, the section which concludes the entire *Anatomy,* melancholy becomes two things. In fact, this doubleness epitomizes what Burton does with melancholy throughout the book, and the structure of the section reflects this doubleness explicitly. For eighty of its 120 pages he treats the causes, symptoms, prognostics, and cures of what he calls "religious melancholy." Then in the final forty pages he goes through the same categories in treating despair. Religious melancholy is one aspect of melancholy considered as metonymic of the human condition, the expression of humanity's alienation from God. Despair is the specific affliction of the individual who cannot believe in the possibility of God's mercy and his own salvation. To enforce a parallel with the discourse on human love, Burton begins the discussion of religious melancholy with a sermon on the beauty of God. Then he concludes the last subsection, "Cure of Despair," with a sermon on the immense mercy of God. This brings the *Anatomy* back to something like what it began with, a specific disease, in this case a spiritual disease, and the cure propounded is similarly a mixture of physic and counsel. Despair is a "mixed disease" and as such must have a mixed remedy (3.4.2.6;3:409,429).

We should expect the treatment of religious melancholy, then, to achieve some of the breadth and geniality of the treatment of love. It does range widely over human religious experience, not only Christian, but Jewish, Islamic, Oriental, and New World. But it is symptomatic of his age that Burton never achieves here the ease or sense of wonder that his earlier rovings over human learning do. Religion was one area where seventeenth-century humanism experienced a constriction of the understanding and sympathy that had prevailed in the earlier Renaissance. The late fifteenth and early sixteenth century had been prepared to see in non-Christian religious experience, both ancient and contemporary, the possibility of analogues and adumbrations of Christian belief. Thomas More's Utopians, whose natural religion both critiques European Christian practice and shares in many of its beliefs, consider it possible that God desires variety in worship and therefore inspired different peoples with different theologies.[17] But the Reformation and the Counter-Reformation effectively put an end to such speculation and made the toleration practiced by the Utopians seem a dangerous aberration. A century of doctrinal polemic and religious war narrowed theological interests down to a handful of disputed points and brought on a dark age that would last into our own century. Non-Christian religions were seen to have nothing to do with a divine predilection for variety but were the inspiration of the devil. And the schisms in the Western Church, of course, were even more fertile grounds for intolerance: each side saw Satan or Antichrist actively at work in the doctrine and practices of its opposition. Burton's discussion of religious melancholy, one may feel, partakes all too much of this theological dark age. What gives the *Anatomy* its general fascination, the ability it has to incorporate the learning and epitomize the attitudes of an entire age, here seems to keep it from the larger vision it promises and to narrow it uncharacteristically. Though we expect some of Sir Thomas Browne's irenicism or speculative generosity, in this respect the divine-turned-physician does not equal the physician-turned-divine.

And yet even failed expectations can prove instructive. In his preface to the third partition Burton quotes a line of Terence that was a favorite tag of Renaissance humanists, "Homo sum, humani a me nihil alienum puto" (I am a man, therefore I count nothing human alien to me) (3.1.1.1;3:8). In the context he is justifying his discussion of love, even though the subject may not seem worthy and he himself has slender experience of the emotion. But the tag seems appropriate to the *Anatomy* generally. Burton's humanism is a kind of anthropology without method; using melancholy as his means, he searches into the various nooks of human experience. This is what we expect him to continue in the discussion of religious melancholy. And he does draw on a wide range of reading about human religious experience. But the search, finally, is marred by a certain negativity as he categorizes non-Christian and indeed non-Anglican practices as superstition. It is clear he does find this experience alien to him, and in the context of the *Anatomy* as a whole this itself seems anomalous.

But Burton's assignment of a cause for superstition is consistent with the humanist ideology of the *Anatomy*. He finds ignorance at the root of all superstition, "their own fear, folly, stupidity, to-be-deplored lethargy, is that which gives occasion to the other, and pulls these miseries on their own heads" (3.4.1.2;3:338). The Mohammedans, he points out, refuse to allow any commentary on the Koran, and the papists "conceal the Scripture" by confining it from the people in Latin and through ignorance "vent and broach all their new ceremonies and traditions" (3:339). And what are the separatists, "Anabaptists, Brownists, Barrowists, Familists," he asks, "but a company of rude illiterate, capricious, base fellows?" Instead of trusting to knowledge, they all enforce their discipline with tyranny over men's minds. In his final sermon against despair Burton quotes lavishly from the Scriptures and the Church Fathers to convey his sense that ignorance of the divine promises of mercy has caused desperation and that knowledge of them will cure it. He thus opposes reading and knowing to solitary meditation, the way perhaps of the mystic, but also of dangerous melancholy.

"Be Not Solitary, Be Not Idle"

There is a kind of paradox in the conclusion of the *Anatomy* which centers on just this understanding. Burton's final word of counsel to the melancholy reader is this: "as thou tenderest thine own welfare in this and all other melancholy, thy good health of body and mind, observe this short precept, give not way to solitariness and idleness." And he repeats, "Be not solitary, be not idle" (3.4.2.6;3:432). But idle solitude is exactly what one must have in order to read, to read the book he has just completed, to read any of the multitude of books the *Anatomy* has gathered and commended. It is what Burton has had to make use of to write his book. But obviously there is a distinction to be made. The apparent idleness of reading is, if the *Anatomy* means anything, the truest activity and exertion. And the solitude required to respond to the written word is only superficial, for the words bring the immediate presence of another mind. Though literally the most solitary of men, Burton's solitude similarly is only a superficial thing, for through the printed word he is constantly in the presence of the twelve hundred and more writers he brings together in the *Anatomy*. And through the printed word the reader as well finds himself in their presence and Burton's. In this way the implicit meaning of Burton's humanism coincides precisely with the best explicit advice he can give the melancholy sufferer. The solipsism, the self-absorption of melancholy is best countered through knowledge, through the community of minds that one encounters in written discourse.

The melancholy we come to understand in the *Anatomy* is not only a specific form of mental and physical suffering, but the very condition of humanity, its folly, self-contradiction, and sinfulness, its failures in love of God and one another. In expanding the sense of melancholy Burton comforts the sufferers from the particular disease by assuring them their condition is universal. "SPERATE MIS-ERI, CAVETE FELICES" are his final emphatic words before he gives Augustine's final counsel of penitence—"You in misery, be hopeful; you who are happy, take care." For melancholy rightly understood is everyone's portion, and no one can evade its suffering altogether. The hope that he holds out rests in what is implicit in every page of the *Anatomy*, that by the activity of searching for knowledge one may avoid the inactivity and self-absorption that breed and maintain melancholy.

It is the searching, finally, that impresses the reader of Burton's book. We lose hope of arriving at any final, stable point of understanding, and by the final partition even the categories represented by the various subsections seem to have broken down. The epistemology of the *Anatomy* remains always provisional. Burton's appetite for the strange, the unexpected, the extreme in human behavior requires leaving room on the library shelves; human knowledge, like his own book, is never definitively completed. Nor is there a definitive cure for melancholy. The final answer to the question of melancholy, like the final answer to the question of jealousy which he coyly withholds from us and promises to whisper in our ear at a next meeting, is never to be found. The only answer, we discover, is the search itself.

Chapter Four
Words against Melancholy

In so long and bookish a book as the *Anatomy of Melancholy* Burton's style is what sustains the reader. He lived his life amid printed words, most of them Latin, but writes an English surprisingly free of the smell of ink and paper. He pretends, in "Democritus to the Reader," that he was forced to write in English because of the greed of "our mercenary stationers" who will print any trash in the vulgar tongue, "but in Latin they will not deal" (1:30). If we believed this, we might be tempted to wonder if he took a revenge of sorts in his curious macaronic prose, English interlarded liberally with Latin. But Burton's English style is so fluent, so accomplished at creating the illusion of a speaking voice, that the vernacular must always have been essential to his project. Though Latin, I shall argue, becomes a kind of ground for his English, enhancing its colloquial tone through contrast, English prose, surely, was always to be his primary antidote to melancholy.

Burton's style is the most significant exception to what I have been describing in the previous chapters as his insistent involvement with printed books and the libraries they made possible. For the voice that we hear in his prose seems precisely that, a voice. "Voice" and "presence" must, of course, remain metaphors when we are speaking (that is, writing) of what is written rather than of what is actually uttered through sound and breath. But through style Burton works to narrow the metaphor to a diminishing point, to render it dead through counterfeiting a spoken voice in written and printed characters.[1] He wishes to compensate not only for the fact of print but also for the consistent bookishness of his method and material. Though the search for a cure for melancholy necessarily locates us amid books, his own language aims at oral presence. Style is a response to the admonition that concludes the book "Be not solitary," for we are never solitary while reading it. He contrives through printed words to create the illusion of speaking endlessly to the reader.

The "Loose" Senecan Style

Burton lived in the great age of experimentation in vernacular prose. In his *Euphues* (1579) John Lyly had taught the English sentence to dance to measured cadences, pointedly antithetical clauses balanced against one another through alliteration and precisely counted syllables. Responding to euphuism in the prose of his *Arcadia*, Sir Philip Sidney rejected the mannered extremes of Lyly's stylistic experiment, but retained the fascination with rhetorical figures as well as the aim of making each sentence a polished structure. Behind both styles stands the dominant Ciceronianism of the sixteenth century, which prized the crafted period built of subordination. But, as Morris Croll has shown, an anti-Ciceronian movement emerged in the late sixteenth century, which took Seneca as a model and aimed at a more rugged, asymmetrical structure.[2] Croll distinguishes two sorts of Senecan style, the "stile coupé" or "curt" style, the primary example of which in English is Bacon's *Essays*, and the "loose style" seen in Burton, Thomas Browne, Donne, and Lancelot Andrewes, among others. The primary goal of the Senecan stylists was to portray not a thought but the experience of thought, a mind in the act of thinking.

But obviously the "loose" Senecan style is a wide net if it can hold such diverse fish. Burton and Browne, for example, share a predilection for asymmetrical sentence structures, elliptical clauses, and suppressed conjunctions. But they shape their sentences differently and employ quite different levels of diction. And each uses Latin in a distinct way. The classic studies of seventeenth-century prose have considered the various practitioners from the perspective of the models they favored.[3] A method that would enable us to distinguish them more fully might instead proceed from the experience of reading. Though both Burton and Browne are conscious Senecan stylists, no one familiar with them would mistake a passage of one for the other. The voice that Browne creates is always more meditative, more intimate, as if he were speaking to a friend who knows his thoughts in general and can be trusted to understand what is not elaborated. Indeed he sometimes appears to be thinking out loud, mildly surprised on occasion at the turn his thoughts take. Surprise and irony are in fact the frequent attributes of Browne's prose. Burton, though he addresses a singular reader, might just as well be speaking to several; his tone is more conversational, even colloquial. Rather than of intimacy, his voice most frequently creates a sense of assurance and genial authority. He is speaking about things he has thought about before, though instances and references come to him as he talks. His irony is either deadpan, or it is evident and closer to sarcasm; he is never himself surprised by it. Though both writers cultivate an impression of improvisation, Burton's syntactic structures are more straightforward. If both wish to portray a mind in the act of thinking, Browne's is the one with more twists and turns. Burton is more obviously addicted to the interpolated Latin phrase, and more apt to quote in Latin, but Browne's diction itself is more Latinate, less homely. A detailed comparison, which is not my intention here, might proceed to define the instances and structures that confirm and qualify what the experience of reading prompts us to expect.

Whenever Burton refers to his own style, it is in terms of negligence and spontaneity. He writes without care or revision, he says, because he has no amanuenses:

I must for that cause do my business myself, and was therefore enforced, as a bear doth her whelps, to bring forth this confused lump; I had not time to lick it into form, as she doth her young ones, but even so to publish it as it was first written, *quicquid in buccam venit* [whatever came to mouth], in an extemporean style, as I do commonly all other exercises, *effudi quicquid dictavit genius meus* [I poured out whatever my mind dictated], out of a confused company of notes, and writ with as small deliberation as I do ordinarily speak, without all affectation of big words, fustian phrases, jingling terms, tropes, strong lines, that like Acestes' arrows caught fire as they flew, strains of wit, brave heats, elogies, hyperbolical exornations, elegancies, etc., which many so much affect. I am *aquae potor* [a water drinker], drink no wine at all, which so much improves our modern wits, a loose, plain rude writer, *ficum voco ficum et ligonem ligonem* [I call a fig a fig and a spade a spade], and as free, as loose, *idem calamo quod in mente* [whatever comes to mind is on the pen], I call a spade a spade, *animis haec scribo, non auribus* [I write these things for the mind, not for the ears], I respect matter, not words; remembering that of Cardan, *verba propter res, non res propter verba* [words for matter, not matter for words], and seeking with Seneca, *quid scribam, non quemadmodum,* rather what than how to write: for as Philo thinks, "He that is conversant about matter neglects words, and those that excel in this art of speaking have no profound learning." (Democritus to the Reader; 1:31–32)

A reader may vacillate between believing and not believing this.

We know, for example, that he did have ample opportunity for revision in the successive editions through which the *Anatomy* went. But in fact he changed little by way of improving the style; either he did not think it worth his while, or he was satisfied with what he had previously written.[4] What he pours out here has much the spontaneity of lively speech; the sentences grow by an accumulation of phrases rather than by carefully plotted subordination. Can the farrago of Latin phrases really have come to him without plan or premeditation? Given Burton's intellectual life, probably so. We rightly suspect *sprezzatura* in any Renaissance writer who protests he pours out extemporaneously whatever comes to mind, and while we hear him protest he writes *animis, non auribus,* we also hear the alliterative play of "fustian phrases" and "caught fire as they flew." He avoids the affectation of big words, he says—like "hyperbolical exornations"? And yet whatever labor may have gone into the composition, the effect is indeed improvisatory and spoken. We notice, particularly in the second sentence, the lack of conjunctions where we would expect to find them and the elliptical grammar, both of which contribute to the impression of a man tossing off phrases to describe himself as nonchalantly as possible.

It is not that Burton is really negligent, of course, but that he aims at the appearance of colloquial negligence. " 'Tis not my study or intent," he protests, "to compose neatly, which an orator requires, but to express myself readily and plainly as it happens." The distinction is between the oratorical style and a *genus humile.* Both are "spoken" styles, but the latter attempts the greater intimacy of a conversational tone. The frequent abruptness contributes to this. In a nearby passage he asks the reader not to contend with him over every point on which he may have erred:

We may contend, and likely misuse each other, but to what purpose? We are both scholars, say,

> *Arcades ambo,*
> *Et cantare pares, et respondere parati.*

If we do wrangle, what shall we get by it? Trouble and wrong ourselves, make sport to others. If I be convict of an error, I will yield, I will amend (1:33).

The longest phrase is seven words long, and most are no more than four or five, the length of a breath. The syntax is straightforward, though it grows ambiguous in "Trouble and wrong ourselves, make sport to others." Following "what" in the previous sentence, "Trouble and wrong" appear at first to be nouns, but followed by "make" could just as easily be verbs with an elided "we shall." To a modern ear the Latin tag gives the passage a studied effect, but the line is Virgil's, a common enough tag from the *Eclogues,* and was ready at hand to describe colleagues. Its own elliptical syntax, moreover, fits into the loose structure of Burton's language in the passage. If the Latin quotations seem to us to add elegancy, Burton's own view was the opposite. A few sentences later he says the practice "makes the style more harsh." The harshness perhaps was heard by a contemporary who was used to speaking Latin in the university and to whom the mixing of the languages may have had the effect of always seeming somewhat ungainly, or at least mildly incongruous.

The passage should be distinguished not only from the oratorical but also from the terse style, the "stile coupé" that Croll counters to the "loose" Senecan style.[5] Burton is obviously not concerned to condense his language here; he spends words as freely as breath. In both the first and the last sentences he repeats verbs not so much to gain clarity as emphasis. In fact, such repetition is a feature of Burton's style generally. It resembles, and may be related to, the practice of doublets in the sixteenth century ("require and charge," for example, in the Prayerbook), in which synonyms were yoked for the sake of clarity, usually from the opposing Anglo-Saxon and Latinate fonts of the language. But Burton redoubles not just words but phrases as well, and in the elaboration adds richness and emphasis rather than clarity. Something similar happens, I want to suggest, when he quotes in Latin, then gives a translation that intends more to paraphrase freely than to render literally.

"This My Macaronicon"

No other seventeenth-century writer I know of makes such insistent use of Latin in his English prose. To account for this and to understand the special quality of Burton's English style, we should see this interpolated Latin as having an essential relationship to the English, a relationship he acknowledges in "Democritus to the Reader" when he calls the *Anatomy* "this my *Macaronicon.*" Latin becomes a ground against which the vernacular can achieve its effects, a linguistic Other of so different a character that its very presence gives his English the peculiar freedom it assumes. By this I do not mean to assert that the Latin is a written, printed medium against which the English can appear spoken. Because virtually no modern readers, even those who can read it well, are likely to speak Latin or comprehend more than a few words aurally, it becomes of necessity for us an almost entirely written code. This was not the case in the seventeenth century; Burton and his university colleagues conversed in Latin and easily understood spoken quotations from Latin writers. When we recall Anthony à Wood's memorial of Burton as unsurpassed in his ability to quote classical authors in his common conversation, we realize the Latin in the *Anatomy* was not in the seventeenth century, as it is likely to be today, a different verbal reality from spoken discourse. It was not a code that depended upon writing for its comprehension but was just as much a part of the oral texture of the prose as the most colloquial passage in English. This needs to be said because to the modern eye the Latin that Burton weaves into his discourse is likely to seem an entirely bookish element. But it too was meant for the ear.

Nevertheless, the Latin quotations do represent difference, a verbal distinction played off against the English. In explaining his style he says that his translations "are sometimes rather paraphrases than interpretations, *non ad verbum* [not literal], but, as an author, I use more liberty, and that's only taken which was to my purpose" (Democritus Junior to the Reader; 1:33). Burton does not, of course, translate all of his Latin quotations and in fact nearly always appears to expect the reader to understand them without help. When he does translate, he usually renders them into a colloquial, racy English whose point is as much difference from the Latin as mere comprehension. For example, in concluding the discussion of love melancholy with the advice to marry, he quotes Philip Beroaldus, a scholar who had scorned marriage, then repented and married:

"For a long time I lived a single life, *et ab uxore ducenda semper abhorrui, nec quicquam libero lecto censui jucundius* [and avoided marrying and judged nothing more pleasant than a bed that is free]. I could not abide marriage, but as a rambler, *erraticus ac volaticus amator"* (to use his own words) *"per multiplices amores discurrebam,* I took a snatch where I could get it; nay more, I railed at marriage downright." (3.2.5.5;3:248–49)

Translation for comprehension is the necessary duty of the modern editor, and my own literal translation, in default of Burton's, is bracketed after the first clause in Latin. But *his* translations here are rather more for the fun of it, the pleasure of moving back and forth between languages, than for the crass necessity of insuring the reader's understanding. After giving Beroaldus's own words (literally, "erratic and inconstant, I ran through a variety of love affairs"), Burton gives his translation: "I took a snatch where I could get it." It both means the same thing and doesn't. "Rambler" precedes Beroaldus's Latin as a rendering of *erraticus*. His *amores* is reduced, amusingly, to "snatch"; the words force Beroaldus from the dignity of polite confession to the locker room. In the lines that follow Burton continues his fun with Beroaldus by turning his Latin into an English of uxorious chirping: "but now [I] recant with Stesichorus, *palinodiam cano, nec poenitet censeri in ordine maritorum,* I approve of marriage, I am glad I am a married man, I am heartily glad I have a wife, so sweet a wife, so noble a wife, so young, so chaste a wife, so loving a wife, and I do wish and desire all other men to marry." This he glosses with Beroaldus's comparatively straightforward "Habeo uxorem ex animi sententia, Camillam Paleoti jurisconsulti filiam" [I have a wife in accord with my wish, Camilla, the daughter of Paleoti the lawyer]. Clearly Burton the bachelor wants to insure that we hear what he has done to poor Beroaldus.

That *hearing* is the heart of it is suggested by another instance of comic translation. Burton checks himself in the midst of a satiric sally: "But I must take heed, *ne quid gravius dicam,* that I do not overshoot myself. *Sus Minervam* [the sow would teach Minerva], I am forth of my element, as you peradventure suppose; and sometimes *veritas odium parit,* as he said 'verjuice and oatmeal is good for a parrot' " (Democritus to the Reader; 1:96). In saying the Latin tag aloud one catches Burton's dotty joke. (It really means "truth breeds hatred," the satirist's motto.) This is an extreme example of his playing one verbal level against another: abstraction turns concrete, a Latin proverb becomes homey advice (albeit of a dubious nature), and meaning is shifted (here, of course, meaning is wholly lost in the play with sound). In another instance Burton goes wholly in the other direction. In considering bloodletting as a cure of melancholy (2.4.3;2:234), he says three main circumstances are to be considered, "Who, how much, when?" This he helpfully glosses as "Quis, quantum, quando?" [who, how much, when?]. Of course,

he is giving a marginal label to his discussion, but one wonders if
he isn't also joking about the literalness, and otiosity, of his translation, even parodying his obsession with the learned language. It
seems all the more likely in that it occurs in the midst of medical
discussion in which the relation between the Latin and his translations is unusually literal and the Latin frequently seems unnec-
essary. In such technical discussions Burton's style flattens out and
we realize how much it depends, at its best, on the witty relation
between Latin and English.

Inkhorn Terms and Doric Dialect

The diction of Burton's English prose shows a similar desire for
contrast to Latin. We would expect that someone who lived his
scholarly life predominantly in the learned language would favor an
inkhorn vocabulary. But in fact Burton uses surprisingly few such
words. A small handful of Latinate terms comprise his self-conscious,
though habitual, use. "Jument" from *jumentum,* is one of these, the
word Burton commonly uses for "cattle." "Diverb" for "proverb"
is another, a word he apparently coined from *diverbium,* the colloquial
speech in a comedy. Others are "explode" (refute or ridicule), "in-
geminate" (reiterate), "colone" (husbandman, from *colonus*), "con-
stringe" (draw together), "perstringe" (censure), "facete" (witty),
"immund" (unclean), "livor" (envy, ill will), "personate" (masked),
and "collogue" (flatter). A slightly larger number occur infrequently:
"clancular" (secret), "exornation" (ornament), "stramineous" (un-
substantial, like straw), "orbities" (bereavements), "obnubilate"
(make obscure), "ambidexter" (double-dealer), "cautelous" (cautious), "calamistrate" (curl the hair), "deliquium" (a faint), "ma-
cerate" (harass), "opiparous" (sumptuous), "vastity" (devastation),
"exolete" (obsolete). These too appear self-conscious usages, though
some may have been common enough at the time and have since
become exolete. Though the list may be more representative than
complete (nor have I included the technical terms from medicine,
science, or astrology), the fact remains that the glossary a modern
reader requires contains a surprisingly small number of learned Lat-
inisms. Only occasionally does a Latinism cause potential misun-
derstanding, as for example the following, which might at first
suggest Burton anticipating a modern psychobiographical theory:
"In the meantime the true Church, as wine and water mixed, lay

hid and obscure to speak of, till Luther's time, who began upon a sudden to defecate, and as another sun to drive away those foggy mists of superstition, to restore it to that purity of the primitive Church" (3.4.1.3;3:369). The surprising verb in the relative clause has its original sense "to purify." He draws an even smaller number of words from Greek for his habitual usage, and most of these are specialized terms: "paraenetical" (in rhetoric, hortatory), "genethliacal" (pertaining to nativities in astrology), "ethnics" (pagans or non-Europeans), "theologasters" (false theologians, analogous to poetasters), "amphibological" (verbally ambiguous). Simple chance dictated that the Latinate "unicorn" would prevail over Burton's Greekish "monocerot," or that so expressive a word as "mormoluches" (from the Greek for a wolfish she-monster) would fail to catch on.

Burton's colloquialism in fact is the more striking and prominent part of his English diction; it is the Burtonian language one is likely to remember. He himself acknowledges—indeed seems to revel in— the charge that his idiom frequently smacks of the streets, that the style is a hodgepodge of high and low:

And for those other faults of barbarism, Doric dialect, extemporanean style, tautologies, apish imitation, a rhapsody of rags gathered together of several dung-hills, excrements of authors, toys and fopperies confusedly tumbled out, without art, invention, judgment, wit, learning, harsh, raw, rude, phastastical, absurd, insolent, indiscreet, ill-composed, indigested, vain, scurrile, idle, dull, and dry; I confess all ('tis partly affected), thou canst not think worse of me than I do of myself. (Democritus to the Reader; 1:26)

"Dizzard" is always his word for a blockhead or generally foolish fellow. A drunk is frequently "fuzzled" in liquor. He warns against marrying a wife who is "snout-fair" alone. Music is a "roaring-meg" against melancholy, that is, a cannon. Travelers are "land-leapers." In the normal course of his writing the colloquial word or turn of phrase is seldom absent for long. When the subject matter calls forth one of his Rabelaisian catalogs, the colloquial impulse fairly takes over. In the following he illustrates the blindness of love:

Every lover admires his mistress, though she be very deformed of herself, ill-favoured, wrinkled, pimpled, pale, red, yellow, tanned, tallow-faced, have a swollen juggler's platter face, or a thin, lean, chitty face, have

clouds in her face, be crooked, dry, bald, goggle-eyed, blear-eyed, or with
staring eyes, she looks like a squis'd cat, . . . a nose like a promontory,
gubber-tushed, rotten teeth, black, uneven, brown teeth, beetle-browed,
a witch's beard, her breath stink all over the room, her nose drop winter
and summer, with a Bavarian poke under her chin, a sharp chin, lave-
eared, with a long crane's neck, which stands awry too, *pendulis mammis,*
"her dugs like two double jugs," . . . a vast virago, or an ugly tit, a
slug, a fat fustilugs, a truss, a long lean rawbone, a skeleton, a sneaker
(*si qua latent meliora puta* [assume better of what's unseen]), and to thy
judgment looks like a mard in a lanthorn, . . . a dowdy, a slut, a scold,
a nasty, rank, rammy, filthy, beastly quean, . . . if he love her once, he
admires her for all this, he takes no notice of any such errors or imper-
fections of body and mind. . . . (3.2.3;3:155–56)

This is Burton the connoisseur of the colloquial, the collector of
slang who obviously took pleasure in the sound of voices scolding
and gossiping. (We may recall the apocryphal story of the amusement he found in walking down the bridge over the Thames to hear
the bargemen swear and suspect there's a truth hidden somewhere
in it.)[6] The lines sketch a Breugelesque picture of extreme human
types, but even more they convey the tone of tavern raillery and
insult, something akin to Falstaff's pleasure in talk for its own sake.
Perhaps *because* he was a man who lived his scholarly life in another
language, Burton had an ear for common speech and knew how to
reproduce it in his prose. This passage calls attention to colloquial
speech, of course, but at nearly every turn in the *Anatomy* Burton
understands the value of the simple Anglo-Saxon word or the commonplace turn of phrase.

The real point of Burton's prose style, I think, is not necessarily
that the colloquial takes precedence over inkhorn or Latinate diction,
but that the wit of his language resides in the way he plays his
English off against Latin. Burton's diction is never so Latinate as,
for example, Milton's. But even if a sentence begins in abstraction,
it is sure to light on something colloquial or Anglo-Saxon by
its end. Consider the following, chosen virtually at random:
"Thus betwixt hope and fear, suspicions, angers, *Inter spemque met-
umque, timores inter et iras,* betwixt falling in, falling out, etc., we
bangle away our best days, befool out our times, we lead a contentious, discontent, tumultuous, melancholy, miserable life"
(1.2.3.10;1:273–74). The line of Horace comes in seemingly to
inflate the rather commonplace abstract words that begin the sen-

tence (and that in anticipation translate the Latin). Then "falling in, falling out," reinforced by the futility in "etc.," deflates that dignity, before "bangle" and "befool" dispel utterly any pretensions to importance our days or times may have and render the polysyllable adjectives a tedious measuring out of life. "Bangle," a word of obscure origin, has to do with hawks beating aimlessly about in the air, but we scarcely need to know this to catch its colloquial tone and hear it, together with "befool," as the rhetorical heart of the sentence.

Through syntax and sentence structure as well we can see Burton playing his English off against Latin. In contrast to the syntactical certainties and firm structure of the Latin sentence, there is a general freedom in the construction of his sentences and a preference for the spoken rhetorical effect over grammatical precision. The grammatical canons of English were not set down until the eighteenth century, so Burton was not violating established rules. Still, Latin made him well aware of precise grammatical structure, and of what he was doing with his English sentences. Rather than frame a structure that depends on subordination, he commonly cobbles his sentences of phrases, often quite short, that appear to tumble out. Antitheses come in short bursts of phrases set against one another:

> To-day we hear of new lords and officers created, to-morrow of some great men deposed, and then again of fresh honours conferred; one is let loose, another imprisoned; one purchaseth, another breaketh; he thrives, his neighbour turns bankrupt; now plenty, then again dearth and famine; one runs, another rides, wrangles, laughs, weeps, etc. (Democritus to Reader; 1:19).

In phrases thus poised antithetically in parallel grammatical structures, he avoids a precisely balanced parallelism of structural units and syllables. "New lords and officers" becomes "some great men," then is altered to the abstract "fresh honours." If he measures "one purchaseth" against "another breaketh" in one clause, he breaks the pattern in the clauses that follow. "One runs, another rides" trails off into the asymmetrical "wrangles, laughs, weeps" that acknowledge the indeterminacy of such listing in the "etc." A sentence frequently seems to be built up as it is spoken, without predetermined structure. This follows the one just quoted:

Thus I daily hear, and such-like, both private and public news; amidst
the gallantry and misery of the world—jollity, pride, perplexities and
cares, simplicity and villainy; subtlety, knavery, candour and integrity,
mutually mixed and offering themselves—I rub on *privus privatus* [my
own private person]; as I have still lived, so I now continue, *statu quo prius*
[just as before], left to a solitary life and mine own domestic discontents:
saving that sometimes, *ne quid mentiar* [not to deceive], as Diogenes went
into the city and Democritus to the haven to see fashions, I did for my
recreation now and then walk abroad, look into the world, and could not
choose but make some little observations, *non tam sagax observator, ac simplex
recitator* [not so much as a shrewd observer than as a simple reporter], not
as they did, to scoff or laugh at all, but with a mixed passion.

The sentence is built initially through appositives, "and such-like"
in apposition to "thus," then "news" in apposition to both. The
prepositional phrase following "amidst," itself structured by apposition, seems to modify "I daily hear," though in meaning it
tends rather to elaborate the sense of "news." But instead it attaches
itself to "I rub on." The sentence turns on the grammatically ambiguous "saving that," participial in form but a conjunction in
meaning. The latter half of the sentence both begins and ends with
clauses expressing analogies, "as Diogenes went," "not as they did";
and the imperfect parallelism of "not . . . to scoff or laugh at all,
but with a mixed passion" concludes the whole. It is scarcely a
model sentence, if by the term we mean a precisely structured
syntactic whole. And yet there is a basic clarity in the way it
develops, oscillating as it does between the private in its main verbs
("I hear," "I rub on," "I continue," "I did walk, look" and so forth),
and the public in its accusatives and adverbial phrases ("news,"
"amidst the gallantry and misery," "fashions," "the world").

"Our Style Bewrays Us"

The verbal pattern most expressive of Burton's mind is one that
elaborates an idea through a series of words and phrases. Rhetorically
it is known as *congeries,* a heaping up. As he habitually piles up
references to learned authorities, so too he piles up verbal structures.
An obvious example is the Rabelaisian blazon of female ugliness
cited above. Another is his alliterated list of nicknames to create an
ubi sunt of beauty:

One grows too fat, another too lean, etc.; modest Matilda, pretty pleasing Peg, sweet-singing Susan, mincing merry Moll, dainty dancing Doll, neat Nancy, jolly Joan, nimble Nell, kissing Kate, bouncing Bess with black eyes, fair Phyllis with fine white hands, fiddling Frank, tall Tib, slender Sib, etc. will quickly lose their grace, grow fulsome, stale, sad, heavy, dull, sour, and all at last out of fashion. (3.2.5.3;3:211)

Sometimes one of Burton's lists can go on and on, as when he catalogs proverbs that express the foolishness of men in "Democritus to the Reader":

To see a fond mother, like Aesop's ape, hug her child to death; a wittol wink at his wife's honesty, and too perspicacious in all other affairs; one stumble at a straw, and leap over a block; rob Peter, and pay Paul; scrape unjust sums with one hand, purchase great manors by corruption, fraud and cozenage, and liberally distribute to the poor with the other, give a remnant to pious uses, etc.; penny wise, pound foolish; blind men judge of colours; wise men silent, fools talk; find fault with others, and do worse themselves; denounce that in public which he doth in secret. . . . (1:67)

And so on, for three pages of text. Inevitably we associate this with the manner in which he develops his points through the constant piling up of quotations and authorities. Such listing, whether pages of proverbial wisdom or the verbal elaboration in a single sentence, is Burton's own form of *copia,* the Renaissance predilection for verbal abundance.

But it is more than an occasional form of playfulness with him, for in briefer, more controlled forms we see it commonly forming his sentences. In these instances the impulse to list fills out the sentence at several syntactic points. Or another way to describe this would be to say that Burton avoids the possible tedium in such listing by shifting his grammatical ground as he lists. The following is a fairly typical example of this. He describes conscience as

A continual testor to give in evidence, to empanel a jury to examine us, to cry guilty, a persecutor with hue and cry to follow, an apparitor to summon us, a bailiff to carry us, a serjeant to arrest, an attorney to plead against us, a gaoler to torment, a judge to condemn, still accusing, denouncing, torturing and molesting. (3.4.2.3;3:401)

Three infinitives follow from "testor," then seven nouns each with one infinitive carry out the metaphor of a legal action. Finally, four participles seem grammatically to modify "a judge," but logically modify the tenor of the metaphor, conscience itself. The sentence is exceptional only in its elaborated metaphor. Aside from this, it demonstrates several common characteristics of his sentence structure. It is built of short phrases, frequently in apposition to one another, and there is an absence of subordinate clauses. No matter that the sentence contains no verb; it is clear and vigorous. And it tumbles out with no conjunctions to mark its progress. His frequent ellipsis is further evident in the way he suppresses the object of several of the infinitives.

Burton's prose shows variation according to his subject matter, from the comparatively flat style of his medical and pharmacological discussions to the exuberance of his satiric flights.[7] But two characteristics remain constant throughout the *Anatomy*: his verbal abundance and the preference for a loose, informal—indeed oral—grammatical structure. Both of these qualities contrast with the Latin that he weaves into his discourse. Latin does not have the richness of vocabulary to compete with the abundance he achieves in his English prose. In fact, a kind of delight in pitting the concision of Latin against the copiousness of English can be seen as a relatively constant feature of the macaronic prose of the *Anatomy*. "In this labyrinth of accidental causes, the farther I wander, the more intricate I find the passage; *multae ambages,* and new causes as so many by-paths offer themselves to be discussed" (1.2.4.7;1:357). The sentence, chosen at random, seems relatively unselfconscious of any effects it may achieve, and for this reason illustrates the point effectively. As we read the sentence we are scarcely aware that the Latin phrase in its center translates, or is a near translation, of three separate phrases in the English that surrounds it, "labyrinth," "more intricate the passage," and "many by-paths." Even less are we likely to be aware that these words come into Burton's English from different linguistic fonts, "labyrinth" from Greek through Latin, "passage" from Latin *(passus)* through French, and "by-paths" from an Anglo-Saxon root. The variety, the *copia,* available in English is obviously a function of its multiple origins, and this is frequently enhanced by the variety of levels of discourse possible in a modern language with its colloquialisms, slangs, and dialects. If Latin is word-poor, it is also concise; it contracts where English expands. It is also well defined in its grammatical structures, while Burton allows his English a certain spoken fluency. One characteristic of several of the examples given here has been the grammatical ambiguity of words and phrases that nevertheless does not cause any lack of clarity in meaning.

In the prose of the *Anatomy* Latin thus becomes the unequal partner of English, the foil against which English can develop its own *copia* and spoken informality. This occurs paradoxically because of the authority Latin held for Burton and his readers. Ninety-five percent of the books in the Bodleian were in Latin.[8] A common feature of vernacular style in the Renaissance, both in prose and verse, is anxiety about its relation to Latin. The vernaculars were parvenus, uncertain of their status in relation to the language in which learning had been expressed for a millenium and a half. And English, it is well to recall, was among the youngest of these upstarts, little more than two centuries old in Burton's time and having experienced the growing pains of transition to its modern form only in the previous century. English, in fact, followed behind Latin, Italian, French, Spanish, Greek, and Hebrew in its representation in the Bodleian.[9] The sixteenth-century treatises that celebrated the vernaculars and their literary use swaggered bravely against this anxiety, but they could not dispel it altogether. The experiments of the Elizabethan poets with quantitative verse are one indication. The fact that all stylistic experiments in prose were modeled on classical examples is yet another. Latin-educated vernacular writers in the sixteenth and seventeenth centuries manifest this anxiety in a variety of ways, in diction, syntax, and stylistics, and in direct proportion, perhaps, to their own learning.

In Burton this anxiety is apparent in the nearly constant presence of Latin within his English prose. Even when he is not quoting, phrases will fall into Latin, as if attracted by a distant but powerful gravitational field exerting force over the writing. Why, then, we might ask, did Burton choose to write the *Anatomy* in English? Why did he not accede to the cultural superiority of the learned language and write, as he says, "more contract in Latin." If we remain skeptical that it was to satisfy a mercenary stationer, one answer would be that he wanted to reach an English audience. This is doubtless true, and the popularity of the book clearly vindicated his choice. But we may still wonder why he did not later bring out a Latin translation and seek an even larger European audience? Instead, he chose for the rest of his life to tinker with—and mostly

add to—his English text. What is there about the style of the
Anatomy that made this inevitable for Burton? As he himself admits,
"It is most true, *stilus virum arguit,* our style bewrays us, and as
hunters find their game by the trace, so is a man's genius descried
in his works" (Democritus to the Reader; 1:27). The traces Burton
leaves us are, predominantly, the verbal abundance and the oral
spontaneity of his style. The oral spontaneity works constantly to
counteract the inherent bookishness of his project—and doubtless
of his life as well. The world of learning in the seventeenth century
was divided between older oral habits of mind and those associated
with written texts. Burton was most emphatically a man of the
book and spent the major part of his life wrapped in the silence of
reading and writing. But to have given himself up to the "more
contract" quality of Latin in the *Anatomy* would have been to yield
altogether to the technology of the library that possessed him. Instead, he chats to us endlessly in a fluent stream of English, ac-
knowledging the claims of Latin in his quotations, but contrasting
to them the freer syntax and verbal richness of vernacular speech.
His style bespeaks a man who would talk of what he has acquired
in the silence of reading. If scholarly melancholy grew in part for
Burton in the contradictions and epistemological relativism that
came in the explosion of printed knowledge, one cure was the vivid
orality of his prose.

Verbal abundance goes hand in hand with the desire for oral
spontaneity. But even more it suggests a mind that thinks by accumulation. Instead of developing his ideas through the logic of
subordination and causal connectives, Burton lists. Parataxis is the
underlying pattern of his prose. Elaboration and qualification come
through the addition of one word, one phrase, one sentence to
another. Sentence typically follows sentence not to express a logical
relation to what has gone before but to provide another, similar
instance or one to contradict what has just been said. Development
occurs in a paragraph through the subtle shifts that occur as clause
follows clause, sentence is tied to sentence. Cause and effect seem
virtually absent from Burton's prose. It reflects a world in which
the connections between phenomena remain indeterminate. Amid
this indeterminacy all one can do is continue enumerating instances.
Leonard Goldstein believes this characteristic comes of Burton's
unconscious reflection of the quantifying tendencies of Galilean science.[10] If so, the relationship is entirely superficial, for it is hard

to imagine a prose less suited to scientific analysis. The force of Burton's language is always centrifugal; he begins with an idea and works out from it through a seemingly open-ended series of analogies and instances. His style resists concentration upon a single point or precise observation. Rarely does he spend more than a sentence or two on an anecdote or in commentary on one of his authorities. When he revises, he adds another phrase, continues his list, elaborates with another sentence or two, includes references to more authors he has read since the last edition.

Burton's style puts the reader into an endless process of discrete observations. Since there seems little hope of making sense of things, the alternative is a continual sorting through of all that concerns human life. Because his prose never stops or concentrates itself to scrutinize a single phenomenon, it implies a consolation to be found in the accumulation of things known. There is, finally, a restlessness at its heart. The frequent *et ceteras* imply the open-endedness of his discourse, but also impatience and an awareness of the impossibility of fixing any limits. What makes this potentially painful activity endurable, and even agreeable, is the voice that engages us, takes us into its confidence, makes us sharers in the process. It is a voice that would not endure being contracted into the concision of Latin but depends on the expansiveness of the vernacular. Through it the text of the *Anatomy,* locked as it is into fixity of print, plausibly imitates a great flow of talk.

Chapter Five

Burton's Minor Works

Apart from the *Anatomy,* all of Burton's other surviving literary activity places him among the Neo-Latin writers of the age. He finds his place, moreover, in a particular subgroup of the Neo-Latinists, the academic, for all his Latin pieces were called forth by particular occasions having to do with the university. *Philosophaster* was produced at the Shrovetide festivities in Christ Church on 16 February 1617, and though Burton says he wrote it some eleven years earlier, its subject matter clearly destined it for academic performance. Twenty of the other Latin poems were written for inclusion in Oxford commemorative volumes, and the one other was a poem praising a colleague's revision of a dictionary and identifying its author by his academic affiliation. As a member of the scholarly community of Christ Church, and well known for his literary accomplishments, he was expected to contribute verses on the occasion of royal visits, births, marriages, and deaths and to commemorate the deaths of other persons important to the university or college. This explains the conventional quality of most of the commemorative verse Burton produced.

Philosophaster

Philosophaster is perhaps the most appealing of Burton's Latin works. It has a liveliness in its representation of university life that redeems its weak plotting and rather flat characterization. Burton was no dramatist, but there is a general exuberance about *Philosophaster* that sets it apart from the rest of his accomplishments in Latin verse. As I noted in chapter 1, the play depends for its effect on the knowing relationship it establishes with its academic audience. Though not a roman à clef, it does play with the notion that the Spanish university of Osuna it portrays does not differ vastly from Oxford. One of the positive characters, Polumathes, has sojourned in Oxford and speaks of his experience in a way calculated to excite wry amusement. And of course its main satiric thrust, that pseudolearned charlatans find a ready haven in a university, is meant to find its general target in Oxford.

University drama represented a tradition not quite a century old in Burton's time.[1] As far as we know, neither Oxford nor Cambridge had contributed much to the rich medieval legacy of vernacular biblical drama; the great cycles of mystery plays were centered on cathedral towns. The writing and performing of plays in the university dates from the latter part of the reign of Henry VIII and was part of the humanist influence on the universities. Play production served two purposes in the colleges. Since the students were in continual residence during the academic year, festivities were a necessity to mark the customary holidays. Christmas gave the dominant occasion for such revelry, but as the Shrovetide performance of *Philosophaster* indicates, other celebratory occasions could call forth plays. The second purpose was to exercise the students in declaiming Latin and to accustom them to speak publicly. For this reason most academic drama was in Latin, though vernacular plays were occasionally produced as well. This latter purpose became the center of the defense of play-giving at the universities when the activity came under Puritan attack late in Elizabeth's reign. Christ Church's William Gager, himself a noted academic playwright, defended the tradition against the learned John Rainolds of Corpus Christi. But the defense of academic play-giving rested finally not so much on learned argument as on royal approval. Both Elizabeth and James attended performances of plays during their visits to the universities, and this was enough to settle the matter.

Burton was concerned to insist in the manuscript of the play that he had written it first in 1606 and that it was only "altered, revised, and completed" in 1615.[2] Well might he insist, for the general situation between Polupistos ("Much-believing") and Pantomagus recalls the central plot of Jonson's *Alchemist,* which was performed in 1610 and printed two years later. One is likely to grant Burton's implicit claim to priority, for the plot idea seems nearly inevitable in dealing with alchemy, and the scenes in *Philosophaster* contain little of Jonson's extravagant imagination. Burton may indeed have taken a hint from Sir Epicure Mammon's speech in constructing Polupistos's similar speech about what he will do with his fabulous wealth, but if so, the relation is in the nature more of imitation than of outright theft. Burton's main defense, unfortunately, would lie in the way he constructs his play. While Jonson delights in setting several plots going at once, then mixing them so the plot lines collide into unexpected comic situations and give his characters scope for new inventiveness, Burton keeps things simple. His scenes are typically short and deal with one plot at a time. As Simon notes, he introduces his characters in separate groups, according to their function and social standing, and with a rather heavy rigidity.[3]

But Burton resembles Jonson in that his satiric villains carry more of the imaginative interest than the positive characters. Indeed, Burton invests his academic charlatans with his own intellectual preoccupations. The central business of the play consists in a group of rogues disguising themselves as respectable academics in order to prey on the university and townspeople. Burton gets his satiric scope from the fact that each professes a different branch of knowledge. Pantomagus is a physician and alchemist, Ludovicus Pantometer a pseudomathematician with an interest (like Burton) in sundials and surveying, Simon Acutus a sophist professing a version of the scholastic philosophy still in use at Oxford, Theanus a rhetorician turned theologian, Amphimacer ("Long-short-long") a Latin poet, and Pedanus a schoolmaster who (also like Burton) takes pleasure in lists of words and (unlike Burton in 1616) acquires a patron and two benefices. The arch-philosophaster is Polupragmaticus ("Much-busied"), "grammarian, rhetorician, geometer, painter, wrestler, soothsayer, rope-dancer, physician, wizard"—or "in a word, a Jesuit" (32–33). To the philosophasters, Burton opposes the genuinely learned Polumathes and Philobiblos. Polumathes in particular, an itinerant humanist and a genuine version of what Polupragmaticus pretends to, becomes Burton's spokesman and satiric persona. What is most significant about Polumathes is that he is so uninteresting, remaining throughout a pale and rather acerbic sort of character. Though he does have an idea for smoking out the philosophasters, his main positive contribution is to prevent the duke of Osuna from disestablishing the university altogether when the pretenders are found out. He is not identified as a melancholic (the word is used several times as if it were an epithet of academic), but he does have something of the melancholy malcontent about him. When Philobiblos questions him about the universities of Europe in the scene in which they are introduced (I. v), we learn that his academic experiences have been entirely negative. He has not met a wise man anywhere, even in Oxford, where the only thing worthy of note seems to be the library; there indeed he found many

of the wise dead, but dressed in chains, and no wise man among
the living:

Phil.   Vidistine veterem Oxoniam?

Pol.   Et instructam illorum bibliothecam, tum in eâ
          Mortuos multos inveni, sed catenis malè habitos
          At vivum illic sapientem vidi neminem.

In another scene (II. v) he rather pedantically questions Theanus
with Philobiblos, but is forced to play straight man to Theanus's
comic ignorance. Something of the same thing happens with Simon
Acutus (III. viii), who spins out a web of mouth-filling jargon,
while Polumathes is reduced to exclamations of frustration. Polumathes' only good scene is V. iv, in which his bitterness reaches
its peak and he denounces all of the academy, especially the academic
theologians ("Tanto crassiores asinos, / Gulae devotos, somno vent-
rique deditos"—"Such stupid asses! slaves to bed and belly"), physicians, and doctors of law. In a manner typically Burtonian, he
stops himself at one point and admits that Osuna has "most learned
men" as well, "whom I revere, esteem, love heartily, and full oft
salute." But they are, he insists, outnumbered by the other sort.

By far the greater inventive power goes into the pretenders to
learning, who frequently remind us of Burton's own interests. When
Polupistos has been robbed of some valuables, he appeals to Polupragmaticus to use his astrological arts to find out the thieves. This
was in fact one of the most common uses of the sort of astrology
Burton himself dabbled in. He does not, of course, mean to satirize
what he would consider legitimate astrological practice, only abuses
and con artists who pretend to astrological expertise. But Polupragmaticus is at least amusing (and not self-deceived) as he goes
about to bilk his victim. When Dromio, Polupistos's clever servant,
threatens to undercut Polupragmaticus with his skepticism, the
latter snatches the initiative and reads Dromio's fortune as a thief
in his palm and face:

          Cave ut dolatas posthac conscendas arbores,
          Ne dimissum lapsus per funem repentè concidas,
          Cadendo collum frangas. Noli altum sapere.

Beware henceforth of climbing upon hewn timbers lest, sliding down the
rope, thou art suddenly slain; the fall may break thy neck. Aspire not to
high things.

(94–95)

In another amusing scene Polupragmaticus gives Simon Acutus advice on how to get ahead in the academic world. He should speak
whenever he gets the chance, publish as much as possible, orations,
epistles, lectures, criticism—no matter what—praise the right people, publish a bibliography of his works with his biography, work
up some extravagant, paradoxical idea, then vehemently attack
whoever criticizes it (IV. ii). Simon decides he'll publish a book
proving the moon is inhabited—by stags and hares, to explain why
dogs always bark at it. (Some twenty years later Burton would
purchase a book attributed to John Wilkins, one of the founders of
the Royal Society, offering to prove the proposition that the moon
was inhabited.)

Above all, the language of the philosophasters is rich with a zany
variety of academic jargons. Amphimacer spouts humanist verse
that sounds at times embarrassingly close to Burton's own conventional effusions. He also frequently quotes the classical poets, including Achilles Tatius, whom Burton's brother William translated.
At times there is an almost Rabelaisian dottiness to the pseudo-
learning assigned to the philosophasters. Simon Acutus expounds
on a passage of philosophy:

Categoriae sunt aves quaedam Macedonicae, rationales, ut canes, et equi;
notate et hoc per viam: et est Graecum, licet scribatur Latinis literis:
notetur et illud valdè *"quae ab Aristotele tradita, etc."* Sic arbitrabar, hic
Aristoteles fuit valdè pauperibus munificus.

Categories are certain Macedonian fowls, having a sense of reason, like
unto that of dogs & horses; note this by the way; 't is all Greek, e'en
though 't was written in Roman letters; and note this especially—"quae
ab Aristotele tradita, &c." . . . which hath been handed down from
Aristotle. Just as I've ever held, this Aristotle was exceeding liberal to the
poor. (60–61)

"Ab Aristotele tradita"—"handed down from Aristotle" or "forked
over by Aristotle"—it's just the sort of play with meaning that
Burton himself relishes in his translations in the *Anatomy*. Similarly

with the jargon Polupragmaticus spouts. When Ludovicus Pantometer worries that the mathematical language will be so obscure
that no one will understand it, Polupragmaticus replies:

> Eo melius. Sic demonstratur quod demonstrandum erat.
> Tuum est disputare de Infinito, Ente, Vacuo,
> Natura naturante, et haecceitate Scoti,
> De causalitate causae, et quidditativa Materia,
> De Gabrielitate Gabrielis, et spiritali animâ.

So much the better. Thus is demonstrated what is to be demonstrated.
It's your job to dispute about the infinite, being, nothingness, Nature
naturing, the thissity of Scotus, the causality of causes, and quidditative
stuff, about the Gabriclity of Gabriel and the soulful spirit. (26; my
translation)

It's all scholastic nonsense, of course, but Polupragmaticus knows
that. The effect is less to induce contempt for him than to make
the audience laugh at the inventive jargon. Another effect, obviously
not part of Burton's explicit design, is to reduce the serious humanists to frustrated straight men. It is not only the notorious
problem that virtue and plain-dealing are harder to make dramat-
ically effective than their opposites. Rather, the case is analogous
to Jonson's comedies where the vehicles of the satire show the greater
investment of imaginative energy. In the case of *Philosophaster* the
invention is mainly verbal, for the action and plotting are minimal.
But the verbal wit remains the province of the pretending rogues.

All but one of the six songs in the play are sung by or at the
behest of the philosophasters. They also contain some of the liveliest
writing—and two of them are arguably among the better of Burton's
Latin poems. This is surprising because, in contrast to his poems
for the commemorative volumes, they are not in classical meters
but in the short rhyming lines of medieval Latin verse. One may
at first suppose that this is an instance of the philosophasters' false
learning, that they compose "gothic" verse rather than the classical
meter a good humanist would favor. But we cannot draw this conclusion because the final song of the play, which celebrates the
overthrow of the "pseudo-academici" and the triumph of good learning, is in the same rhymed verse. (Burton notes, in English, that
the song is to be sung "To the tune of Bonny Nell.") There is not
much to the first song that Simon Acutus is assigned to sing at the

close of act 3. But the next song, which Aequivocus sings for
Antonius at the window of Camaena, has at least a novel idea in a
lover's serenade:

> Pungens procul esto pulex,
> Cantans procul esto culex . . .
>
> Keep away, you biting flea,
> Buzzing gnat, away with thee . . .
>   (148; my translation)

Theanus sings a farewell to the university that has the vigor of a
good drinking song. It has, moreover, the virtue of easy adaptability
to Oxford use. In its first stanza,

> Valete Academici,
> Et combibones optimi,
> Osunensesque reliqui,
>   Et nunc et in perpetuum!
>
> Farewell, ye Academic louts,
> And toss-pots of dear drinking bouts,
> Townsfolk, and all who heard our shouts
>   Both now and evermore! (158–60)

Osununsesque could obviously be turned to *Oxoniensesque*. And the
churches in stanza 3 belonged to Oxford as well as to Osuna:

> Sancte Petre in occidente,
> Sancte Petre in oriente,
> Cum Mariâ mediante,
>   Et nunc et in perpetuum! (160)

The university church of St. Mary's stands about halfway between
St. Peter's in the East and St. Peter le Bailey (the latter now a part
of St. Peter's College). Did "Valete Academici" become a Christ
Church favorite? Another drinking song, in its vigor strongly reminiscent of the student songs found in medieval collections, closes
act 4. It too is in accentual meter and the rhymed stanza found in
a number of these collections:

Exultemus et ovemus,
Pergraecemur et potemus
Simul et amicè.

Let us revel and rejoice,
Let us drink and sing,
Let's resound with lifted voice,
Together let it ring. (178–79)

Perhaps the best of the songs is the one that precedes this, a brief (three-stanza) retelling of Phoebus's discovery of Mars and Venus and Vulcan's netting them flagrante delicto:

Phoebus dum pererrat orbem,
Lustrans quaeque, praeter spem
Martem videt et Venerem,
Sine thalamo cubantem,
At nec Phoebus visum celat,
Sed Vulcano rem revelat.

As Phoebus swept along his way
Replacing friendly night with day,
He spied where Mars and Venus lay;
They clip't upon a couch defiled,
So Phoebus peeped and, lo! he smiled,
Then sped for Vulcan to betray.

After each of the three stanzas, a comic refrain is sung by all:

Ex Diis quidam tum facetè,
O utinam vidisset me,
Cubantem sic cum Venere.

One of the gods then merrily cried:
Would that he had seen but me,
Bedded thus at Venus' side!

Vidisset (saw) becomes *ligasset* (bound) and *ridisset* (laughed at) in the second and third refrains. One would not want to make great claims for it, but the poem has an amusing lightness reminiscent of Herrick.

The Commemorative Verse

Burton's Latin verse which appeared in the commemorative volumes has been faulted by the few readers it has found for its me-
diocrity and conventionality. Jordan-Smith says he is aware of his
understatement when he pronounces it "not of the best."[4] Simon
speaks of the absence of emotion hiding under the mask of grandiloquence and an aridity of inspiration behind a constant appeal
to astrological imagery.[5] Burton would be unlikely to understand
the charge of insufficient emotion, for the subjects of most of them
were personally unknown to him. Of the twenty-one poems fourteen
are concerned with the royal family.[6] The grandiloquence, moreover,
is a function of Burton's models, the silver-age Roman poets rather
than the Augustans. Hyperbole, elaborate conceits, farfetched mythological or historical references (and also some fairly obvious ones)
go hand in hand with his use of astrology to establish the poems
as stylistic imitations of silver-age verse. None of these elements
commend themselves much to modern taste, nor in fact are we likely
to know the verse of Seneca, Lucan, Martial, or Statius as well as
that of Virgil, Ovid, Horace, or Catullus. But they were very much
a part of the aesthetic of early seventeenth-century Latin verse.
Conventionality is a charge that Burton would be likely to take
rather as a compliment. The conventions are those that link the
verse to imperial Roman poetry and therefore implicitly link their
political subjects to Roman counterparts. The best stylistic analogies
to Burton's poems may be Rubens's allegorical paintings of James
and Charles in the Banqueting House of Whitehall, in which the
monarchs are attended by personifications and classical gods and
goddesses. Poem XI, in fact, imagines a scene of abstract personifications attending the tomb of James; it is not one of Burton's more
successful performances, but rather because of its rhetorical flat-
footedness than because of conventionality.

Burton's poems ask to be judged as examples of political praise
rather than as expressions of feeling. Usually the poems have a single
idea in them, which is either worked out wittily, or fails by over-
elaboration or rhetorical flatness. Poem VI, celebrating James's return from his Scottish visit of 1617, is an example of a relatively
successful piece of political praise. Burton's main conceit is that
England and Scotland are separated by Hadrian's Wall as the equator
separates the southern and northern hemispheres. Thus, though the

sun shines on each at the same time, each experiences the opposite season. He uses the learned word *antoeci* from a Greek root, "opposed as by a meridian," to express this idea of geographical opposition. James is the sun who shines equally on both kingdoms, even though they are separated by their laws and traditions of governance. But when the king travels north to Scotland, his rays shine obliquely on England, which then suffers winter while Scotland enjoys a summer of festival. And James's return brings summer back to England and leaves Scotland cold and desolate. The poem ends with an allusion to Psalm 19, the sun as a bridegroom coming forth from his chamber like a strong man to run his race, that the poem identifies with James. It is not a conceit worthy of Donne at his best, but it has for Burton's purposes the utility of expressing political doubleness within a united kingdom and of employing again the well-used but politically potent symbol of the sun for the monarch. The conceit also has the advantage of clarity, after one understands what he means by *antoeci,* and gives him scope to develop conventional seasonal imagery. Though the longest of Burton's poems (fifty-four lines), it attains a kind of qualified success as a piece of competent political praise.

Burton's astrological conceit that he used to mark the royal visit of 1605 has similar success in briefer compass. Here he takes note of the astrological conditions of the time of the visit and records that the sun was joined with Venus and Mercury in the house of the Virgin. This he interprets, or rather projects, as the King joined with the Queen and Prince Henry who would stay in Christ Church:

> Soli juncta Venus, Veneri Cyllenius heros,
>   Virginis inque unâ parte, quid esse putem?
> Sol Rex, et Venus est Regina, Ecclesia Virgo,
>   Mercurius Princeps, quid mage perspicuum?
> Sic, ô sic veri semper praesagia coeli
>   Sidera, venturos significate Deos.
> Et quoties fuerit Veneri Sol Virgine junctus,
>   Atlantis magni Pleionesque nepos:
> Dignetur toties tua nos praesentia, et aedes
>   invise has toties (magne *Jacobe*) tuas.

Venus is joined to the Sun, Mercury to Venus, and all in the single house of the Virgin. What am I to make of this? The Sun is the King, Venus is the Queen, the Virgin is Christ Church, Mercury is the Prince—what could be more obvious? Thus, o thus, presaging stars of heaven, do you signify to us the visiting Gods. And so oft as the Sun shall be joined to Venus with the Virgin and the Pleionian nephew of great Atlantis (i.e., Mercury), so oft shall your presence be granted us, and so oft may you, great James, visit your college.[7]

The poem ends with four more lines that leave the conceit behind and conclude somewhat lamely. If we are inclined to smile at Burton's rhetorical question "quid mage perspicuum?" we can be sure that he did too. Of course, the conceit is farfetched, just as farfetched as calling Mercury the Cyllenian hero and the Pleionian nephew of Atlantis. Both are a part of the heightened stylistics of the poem, one that values preciosity over the obvious. If Burton is to be faulted for anything in these lines, it is the somewhat flat linking of tenor to vehicle in line three.

In fact, only one other of Burton's poems uses astrology as the basis of a conceit. His poem on the death of Prince Henry (III) takes note of the fact that five of the seven planets were hidden at the hour of his death, and only the baleful Saturn and Mars were in the heavens. Either the five planets hid themselves so they would not see so sad an event, or death took advantage of their absence to strike his blow. Because each star is also a god, Burton is able to mythologize their absence into shame at not being able to grant the gifts that each had promised Henry. And so each compensates by offering a gift in death. The poem is less successful than the previous one using an astrological conceit because of its length and the fact that Burton must find something for all five gods to do. In a serious poem, moreover, the conceit has to be taken more seriously, and this overtaxes its powers.

In his elegy for the death of the noted Greek scholar and mathematician Sir Henry Savile (VIII) Burton makes use not of astrology but of the astronomical tradition that named the constellations:

> Suspicio quoties signis variabile coelum,
>   Zodiacum obliquum, stelliferumque polum;
> Hinc video fera monstra, illinc animalia, pisces,
>   Inde canes, lepores, praestigiasque hominum,
> Informes ursos, aurigas, plaustra, dracones . . .

As often as I look upon the constellations of the sky, the slanting zodiac and the star-bearing pole, I see on one side wild monsters, on the other animals and fish, there dogs, rabbits, and deceptive images of men, shapeless bears, charioteers, wagons, dragons . . .

Why such strange and monstrous forms, he asks; is it Ptolemy's doing or the imperious power of poets that has imposed this on us? He prefers the tradition that has named constellations for mythical heroes, "*Perseus*[,] *Alcides, Cephesus,* divinus *Orion,* / Cum *Geminis Cheiron,* pulcher et Antinous" (Perseus, Hercules, Cephesus, divine Orion, with the Twins, Cheiron, and beautiful Antinous), who were all once illustrious astronomers, he says. Then let the wandering crowd of monsters come down from the skies, and let a new cohort of heroes, one "worthy of Jove," hold their place: "Alphonsus, Bacon, Ticho, Copernicus alter / Atlas, Candisius, Drakus et Americus." Savile too will have his star amid this company of extraordinary explorers of the cosmos. Because Savile, besides being a distinguished scholar himself, had endowed professorships of geometry and astronomy at Oxford, there is a propriety in Burton's conceit. He at first assigns the imaginative task of stellification to a poet ("O si quis vates nostro floreret in aevo" [O if any poet flourishes in our age]), as Ovid had translated the shade of Caesar to the skies, but rejects this possibility and instead asserts that the Muse herself will give him an eternal name. In the Neo-Latin tradition the Muse means not simply poetry but learning in general, so Burton's distinction means that Savile need not depend on anything beyond the work he has himself accomplished for the fame he leaves behind. The compliment is nicely turned, and the poem has one of Burton's more graceful conclusions. Again the poem has no discernible emotion—perhaps Burton was acquainted with Savile, but probably little more. Grief is scarcely its point, but rather to project imaginatively something of Savile's significance in the world of learning. Savile has been one of those *Solis quondam comites* (sometime companions of the Sun) who have shed light on what is in the cosmos with their rays. Burton's word *radiis* for rays wittily means measuring instruments as well. Approached in terms of the occasion it was designed for, the poem seems entirely successful.

But not all of Burton's academic commemorations were as successful. The poem he contributed to the volume for Camden in 1624 begins rather lamely by quoting five lines that Camden had written years before for Roger Ascham. The next nine lines simply apply the same praises to Camden. More amusing at least is the poem Burton wrote for the third edition of his friend Francis Holyoke's revision of John Rider's Latin-English Dictionary. (Burton also contributed a preface to the second edition of Holyoke's revision of

John Rider's *Dictionarie* (1612); the poem appeared in the 1617
edition.) He begins with some extended playing with Holyoke's
names. No doubt our tastes run less to such punning on names.[8]
But there is an amusing extravagance to Burton's wit. The forest
of Arden, Holyoke's birthplace, is now equal to Dodona in bringing
forth "sacras quercus." And as the oaks of Dodona bear acorns, so
Holyoke has brought forth many etymologies to scholars' use. The
carpenter fashions many things of oak, and Holyoak is no less distinguished a carpenter of words, filling not only dictionaries with
words, but his sermons as well. May the Muse make him a crown
of oak leaves, the poem asks, that he may wear without end. In the
second half of the poem Burton drops the puns and develops the
conceit of his friend as a Hercules-like tamer of monstrous words,
or a restorer of decay-eaten words from the Hydra that oppresses
them. Mythological extravagance replaces verbal extravagance.

Not surprisingly, Burton's most successful commemorative poems
are the three he composed to mark the death of Thomas Bodley in
1613. It has gone unnoticed that these are imitations of the first
three poems of Martial's *De Spectaculis Liber,* which celebrate the
building of the Flavian Amphitheater (or Colosseum).[9] Burton in
fact begins and ends his first poem with the lines of Martial's first
poem, which he italicizes to emphasize that he is quoting:

> *Barbara Pyramidum sileat miracula Memphis*
>   Aut olim quicquid *Roma* superba dedit.
> Et *Sophiae* templum Bizantia littora longè,
>   Jactare hinc cessent *Justiniane* tuum.
> Ostentare suum Veneti, et *Nidrosia* templum
>   Desinat, aut *Aedes Escoriale* suas.
> *Argentina* suas taceat *Cremonaque* turres,
>   *Hispalis* à Mauro coctile celet opus.
> Omnis enim nostro cedat structura *Lyceo,*
>   *Unum pro cunctis fama loquatur opus.*

Let barbaric Memphis fall silent about the wonders of the Pyramids, or
whatever proud Rome has given. Let the far-off Byzantine shores cease
boasting, Justinian, of your temple of Hagia Sophia. Let the Venetians
stop showing their temple, Nidrosia hers, and the Escorial its courts. Let
silvery Cremona grow dumb about its towers, and Seville hide its Moorish
brickwork. For every building must yield to our Lyceum, and Fame must
speak of one work in place of all.

Burton replaces Martial's wonders of the ancient world with ones he knows from the modern world. To make good the claim in the final line, he needs the final poem, which also begins with a version of Martial's first line *"Quae tam seposita est, quae gens tam barbara voce"*—what race so remote, so barbarous of speech. The Roman poet had asked what people was so remote that it did not send spectators to the great amphitheater. The Oxonian asks what people and what language are so remote that the library does not contain one of their books. Whatever the Indians, Arabs, Greeks, Latins, Ethiopians, Persians, Hebrews or Syrians have given in the ancient world, or whatever the French, Italians, Spaniards in the modern vernaculars, all this Bodley has collected. It is not so much an architectural feat, as the first poem might lead us to suppose, but rather the cultural wonder that Burton celebrates. This, implicitly, is the wonder that equals the Colosseum. For once, the hyperbole proves to be literal fact when the poem predicts that the walls that Bodley has refurbished will always resound his name: "Aeternumque tuum resonabunt moenia nomen."

The second poem of the series ends with a version of Martial's final couplet: "Reddita Roma sibi est et sunt te praeside, Caesar, / deliciae populi, quae fuerant domini" (Rome has been returned to herself and with you presiding, Caesar, that delight is now the people's that was once their master's). This Burton turns into "Reddita Musa sibi est Bodleio Praeside, fiunt / *Deliciae populi quae fuerant domini*" (The Muse is returned to herself and with Bodley presiding, that delight has become the people's that was once their master's). The poem contrasts the former squalor of what Duke Humphrey's library had become with what Bodley has made of it. The barbarism of spiders, cockroaches, moths has given way to gilded beams and a painted ceiling, and now the books stand in comely order, each Muse entrusted to her proper rank. Taken together, the three poems are an impressive example of *imitatio,* a witty adaptation of verbal structures from the Roman world to Burton's Oxford. As I have been suggesting, much of their meaning resides precisely in this adaptation. The same language and verse pattern, indeed the same stylistic assumptions, serve poets separated by a millenium and a half. The Bodleian is scarcely the imperial architectural marvel the Colosseum is, but Burton invests it with something of a claim for similar cultural universalism.

Conclusion

Burton's Latin poetry shows us some significant sides of him we would not know from the *Anatomy*. While *Philosophaster* has satiric aims in common with the major work, it also shows us its author entering the high spirits of a college festival. The town/gown jokes, the foolery of the academic jargon, the drinking songs, all outweigh the seriousness invested in Burton's spokesman in the play. Since he says he wrote the play in 1606, we might suppose that it reflects a period of literary activity before the major work on the *Anatomy*, when he was in his late twenties. When the play was produced, he had just turned forty and was no doubt deep in his researches for the *Anatomy*. But he was far from being the formidable author of that book and the crochety elder statesman of Christ Church. Rather he was immersed in college and university duties as well as in his own studies, and the play suggests something of the spirit in which he fulfilled them. The Democritus Junior of the *Anatomy* is not perhaps the first person one would call on for a Shrovetide play, but *Philosophaster* shows us a younger don who takes the university seriously, but not too seriously. The Latin verse in the commemorative volumes at its best illustrates Burton's ability at imitation of classical verse. We see his awareness of the stylistics of silver-age poetry, and his ability to fashion conceits in that tradition. Even if we cannot quite speak of his mastery of the form of the short poem, his poems demonstrate a craftsmanship that suggest what he might have done if he had devoted himself to the lyric rather than to the prose of the *Anatomy*. For the poems on subjects that capture his imagination, especially those commemorating Bodley's accomplishment, show more than competence in adapting classical models to contemporary use. The author of the very different prose of the *Anatomy*, we learn, has a surprising ability in adapting Latin elegiac verse to the epigram.

But inevitably the minor works in Latin throw into relief the accomplishment of the *Anatomy* and make us see how much Burton's genius depended on the expansive, dilating format of his major work. He appears at his best in the short poems when he has a classical model to imitate. Failing that, the sense of form becomes less certain, particularly, perhaps, in *Philosophaster*. But in the *Anatomy* he goes in the opposite direction from the sort of concentration required by lyric and drama. The relaxation of formal restrictions seems to free him in every way. So much of the appeal of the *Anatomy* depends upon this freedom. We never know where Burton will turn next as his prose talks on and on, citing authorities, giving instances, happening upon curiosities at every turn. Whatever claims may be made for its structure, the *Anatomy* is clearly one of the "loose baggy monsters" of our literature. What renders it so eminently readable is our sense that anything may turn up in its encyclopedic pages. Burton too felt that its claims rested on plenitude, and he was impelled continually to add to its immensity, not to shape it into something more comely. It is one of those books that persuade us that everything somehow must be contained in its pages, like Borges' "Book of Sand," which can be concealed only in an immense library.[10] So too the prose of the *Anatomy* stands at the opposite pole from the concision of Latin verse. It requires the openness of the vernacular, the sense that there is no limit to where words may be gathered from. In the comedy Burton presses Latin hard to find language sufficiently zany for his philosophasters. But to create the fluent prose of the *Anatomy,* he needed English with its multiple fonts and its resources in colloquial speech. And he needed Latin as well to set off his English, to give it a foil sufficient to emphasize its rhythms and energy. For the real character of the *Anatomy* is its inclusiveness. It could not stop growing while its author was alive. Unlike a lyric poem, "Burton's Melancholy," as the seventeenth century called it, was continuous with its author. It knew what he knew, expanded to match the progress of his reading, cataloged his doubts, changes of mind, convictions, and prejudices. Is there any other book, one wonders, that absorbed so much of its author's life—and continues to express so fully a life bounded by books?

Notes and References

Chapter One

1. Jean Robert Simon's "Esquisse d'une biographie" is the closest there is to a standard biography, *Robert Burton (1577–1640) et l'Anatomie de la Melancholie* (Paris: Didier, 1964), 11–58. This is supplemented by Richard L. Nochimson, "Studies in the Life of Robert Burton," *Yearbook of English Studies* 4 (1974):85–111, and several recent biographical notes cited below.

2. Burton noted the day and hour of his conception and birth in his copy of Joannes Stadius's *Ephemerides* (Cologne, 1581). His nativity is contained in manuscript notes in Bodleian 4°.R.9.Art, a volume which contains Ptolemy's *Quadripartum Iudiciorum Opus* (Paris, 1519), John Dee's *Propaedeumata Aphoristica* (London, 1558), and Cyprian Leowitz's *Brevis et Perspicua Ratio Iudicandi Genituras* (London, 1558). This volume is described in detail by J. B. Bamborough, "Robert Burton's Astrological Notebook," *Review of English Studies* n.s. 32 (1981):267–85.

3. Bamborough, "Astrological Notebook," 274–79. For a full discussion of Burton's nativity, see E. Patricia Vicari, "Saturn Culminating, Mars Ascending: the Fortunate/Unfortunate Horoscope of Robert Burton," in *Familiar Colloquy: Essays Presented to Arthur Edward Barker,* ed. Patricia Brückmann (Ontario: Oberon Press, 1978), 96–112.

4. Vicari, "Saturn Culminating," 105–6.

5. The manuscript is Bodleian MS Marshall 132. It bears the inscription "Ceo est le lyvre Gylyalm Burton iadys le porter del Baner royal notre sire le Roy Henri d'Engleterre" ["le sixièsme" in later hand].

6. According to the manuscript, Mary was born 13 July 1578; George, 28 August 1579; Jane, 17 October 1580; Ralph 3 July 1582; and Catherine, 22 October 1584.

7. See Simon, *Robert Burton,* 18–19.

8. Simon, *Robert Burton,* reproduces the engraving, 14.

9. William Burton, *The Description of Leicestershire* (London, 1622), 174.

10. Simon, *Robert Burton,* 19–20.

11. William Burton, *Description,* 105–6.

12. Laurentius Arturus Faunteus, *Apologia libri sui de inuocatione ac veneratione sanctorum* (Cologne, 1589); the copy is Bodleian 8°.A.71.Th. William Burton gives a different date for this uncle's death, 1591.

13. Roger Ascham, *The Scholemaster,* ed. R. J. Schoeck (Don Mills, Ont.: J. M. Dent, 1966), 24–25.

14. C. E. Mallet, *A History of the University of Oxford* (New York: Longmans, 1924), 2:2–9, 17.

15. Mark H. Curtis, *Oxford and Cambridge in Transition, 1558–1642* (Oxford: Clarendon, 1959), 54–82.

16. Anthony à Wood, *Athenae Oxonienses* (London, 1815; reprint, 1967), 2:652.

17. Barbara H. Traister, "New Evidence about Burton's Melancholy," *Renaissance Quarterly* 29 (1976):66–70. My account of Forman's consultations with this young Robert Burton follows Traister.

18. Wood, *Athenae Oxonienses,* 2:652.

19. Cuddesdon had a short life; it was burned down by the royalist governor of Oxford in 1644 to prevent its use as a garrison by the Parliamentary forces. It was rebuilt in 1679 by Bishop John Fell, the son of Burton's friend Samuel Fell, dean of Christ Church.

20. Simon, *Robert Burton,* 24.

21. Curtis, *Oxford and Cambridge,* 79–81, 107–114.

22. Paul Jordan-Smith, *Bibliographia Burtoniana; a Study of Robert Burton's The Anatomy of Melancholy* (Stanford: Stanford University Press, 1931), 9.

23. The accession volume was *Academiae Oxoniensis Pietas erga Iacobum Regem* (Oxford, 1603); *Musa Hospitalis, Ecclesiae Christi, Oxon.* (Oxford, 1605) celebrated the royal visit. The twenty-one occasional poems, all in Latin, Burton wrote for such volumes are collected in *Burton's Philosophaster and Other Minor Writings,* ed. Paul Jordan-Smith (Stanford: Stanford University Press, 1931), 247–71.

24. Nochimson, "Studies in the Life of Burton," 97; see also Richard L. Nochimson, "Robert Burton's Authorship of *Alba*: a Lost Letter Recovered," *Review of English Studies* n.s. 21 (1970):325–31.

25. Philip Stringer's report on the performance is quoted by Nochimson, "Burton's Authorship of *Alba*," 328. See also E. K. Chambers, *The Elizabethan Stage* (Oxford: Clarendon, 1923), 1:130.

26. The play is printed in *Robert Burton's Philosophaster,* ed. and trans. Paul Jordan-Smith.

27. Mallet, *History of Oxford,* 312–14, 333–34; see also V. H. H. Green, *A History of Oxford University* (London: B. T. Batsford, 1974), 73–75, 81–82.

28. See Henry L. Thompson, *Christ Church,* University of Oxford College Histories (London, 1900), 35–39.

29. John Aubrey, *Brief Lives,* ed. Oliver Lawson Dick (London: Secker & Warburg, 1949), 72.

30. Mallet, *History of Oxford,* 90–91; on the library's refounding by Bodley, see 213–30.

31. W. G. Hiscock, *A Christ Church Miscellany* (Oxford: Oxford University Press, 1946), 3–7.

32. Burton refers to himself as "Keeper of our college library" in a note to his appreciation of Oxford's libraries in "Democritus Junior to the Reader," 1:17).

33. Hiscock quotes a portion of the oath: ". . . Itemque neque ego in persona mea neque quisquam olim me authore, consciove, palam aut occulte, surripiendo, permutando, radendo, deformando, lacerando, scindendo, annotando, interscribendo, sponte corrumpendo, obliterando, contaminando, aut alio quocumque modo detruncando . . ." *Christ Church Miscellany,* 7.

34. See S. Gibson and F. R. D. Needham, "Lists of Burton's Library, *Oxford Bibliographical Society: Proceedings and Papers* 1 (1922–26):222–46. Professor Nicholas Kiessling has recently compiled a more accurate and up-to-date listing of the contents of Burton's library, which will be published by the Oxford Bibliographical Society in 1986. The statistics I cite, including the percentages of the categories of the library, come from his tabulations, and I am grateful to him for making his researches available to me.

35. On the volume, see above, note 2.

36. Bamborough, "Astrological Notebook," 280.

37. Michael MacDonald notes a similar caution in Richard Napier, an astrological physician and also a clergyman, *Mystical Bedlam: Madness, Anxiety and Healing in Seventeenth-Century England* (Cambridge: Cambridge University Press, 1981), 21–26.

38. White Kennett, *Register and Chronicle* (1728; 1744 ed.), 320–321. Babb points out that there were no barges as high as Oxford until 1635, *Sanity in Bedlam,* 31n.

39. Jordan-Smith, *Bibliographia Burtoniana,* 10–11; see also Nochimson, "Studies in the Life of Burton," 96–97.

40. Simon, *Robert Burton,* 35.

41. The Puritan *Admonition to Parliament* (1572) had earlier complained of the use of wafers instead of "common and usual bread" for the sacrament. In the seventeenth century Puritan influence caused bread to be used instead of wafers (Horton Davies, *Worship and Theology in England* [Princeton: Princeton University Press, 1 (1970):266; 2 (1975):305]).

42. Jordan-Smith, *Bibliographia Burtoniana,* 8–9.

43. Lady Frances's predecessor, one John Conyers, had reduced the acreage of the living from 28 acres to 19. Burton brought suit on 15 September 1626, and was granted his nine acres five days later (Simon, *Robert Burton,* 35).

44. Karl Josef Höltgen, "Robert Burton and the Rectory of Seagrave," *Review of English Studies* 27 (1976):129–36.

45. Höltgen discovered the incident and describes it, ibid., 135.

46. The letter, dated 7 August 1635, is British Library Add. MS 49381. The text was printed by T. C. Skeat, "A Letter of Robert Burton," *British Museum Quarterly* 22 (1960):12–16.

47. Wood, *Athenae Oxonienses*, 2:652–53.

48. "Pondus verborum trutino, / Affectus moveo, Suadae medullam exerceo," *Philosophaster*, 34–35.

49. Wood, *Athenae Oxonienses*, 2:653.

50. Jordan-Smith prints the will, *Philosophaster*, 275–78.

51. W. K. Jordan, *Philanthropy in England: 1480–1660* (London: Allen & Unwin, 1959), 16–17, quoted in Nochimson, "Studies in the Life of Burton," 108.

52. John Aubrey, *Brief Lives*, ed. Andrew Clark (Oxford, 1898), 1:130.

53. Wood, *Athenae Oxonienses*, 2:653.

54. Nochimson, "Studies in the Life of Burton," 108.

55. See Nicholas Dewey, "Burton's Melancholy: a Paradox Disinterred," *Modern Philology* 68 (1971):292–93.

56. Quoted by Nochimson, "Studies in the Life of Burton," 108.

57. See Vicari, "Saturn Culminating," 107–8.

Chapter Two

1. Nicholas Dewey notes that the title of Burton's book was abbreviated *Melancholy* in the seventeenth century rather than *Anatomy*, as it is now; early readers thus defined it by its subject rather than by its method ("Burton's *Melancholy*," 292–93).

2. Wood, *Athenae Oxonienses*, 2:653.

3. See Paul Jordan-Smith, *Bibliographia Burtoniana*, 107.

4. James Boswell, *Life of Johnson*, Everyman ed. (London: J. M. Dent, 1949; reprint, 1962), 1:389.

5. Sir William Osler, "Burton's *Anatomy of Melancholy*," *Yale Review* 3 (1914):251–71; Bergen Evans, *The Psychiatry of Robert Burton* (New York: Columbia University Press, 1944); William R. Mueller, *The Anatomy of Robert Burton's England* (Berkeley: University of California Press, 1952).

6. Rosalie Colie, *Paradoxia Epidemica: the Renaissance Tradition of Paradox* (Princeton: Princeton University Press, 1966), 430–60; Joan Webber, *The Eloquent "I": Style and Self in Seventeenth-Century Prose* (Madison: University of Wisconsin Press, 1968); Stanley E. Fish, *Self-Consuming Artifacts: the Experience of Seventeenth-Century Literature* (Berkeley: University of California Press, 1972), 303–52; Ruth A. Fox, *The Tangled Chain: the*

Structure of Disorder in the Anatomy of Melancholy (Berkeley: University of California Press, 1976).

7. Translated as *A Discourse of the Preservation of the Sight: of Melancholike diseases; of Rheumes, and of Old Age* (London, 1599).

8. Douglas Bush, *English Literature in the Earlier Seventeenth Century, 1600–1660* (Oxford: Clarendon Press, 1945; rev. ed., 1962), 296.

9. On Burton and Montaigne, see especially J. B. Bamborough, "Burton and Cardan," in *English Renaissance Studies Presented to Dame Helen Gardner in Honour of her Seventieth Birthday*, ed. John Carey (Oxford: Oxford University Press, 1980), 189–92.

10. See Elizabeth Eisenstein, *The Printing Press as an Agent of Change* (Cambridge: Cambridge University Press, 1979), esp. 73–78 and 518–19; and Walter Ong, S.J., *The Presence of the Word: Some Prolegomena for Cultural and Religious History* (New Haven: Yale University Press, 1967), 272.

11. François Rabelais, *The Histories of Gargantua and Pantagruel*, trans. J. M. Cohen (Baltimore: Penguin, 1955; reprint, 1963), 194.

12. Wood, *Athenae Oxonienses*, 2:653.

13. Eisenstein, *The Printing Press*, 74.

14. Devon L. Hodges, *Renaissance Fictions of Anatomy* (Amherst: University of Massachusetts Press, 1985), 6, 15, 18.

15. Ibid., 121.

16. Webber, *The Eloquent "I,"* 94.

17. Jorge Luis Borges, *Labyrinths* (New York: New Directions, 1964), 65.

18. Fox, *The Tangled Chain*, 5, 22–30.

19. Ibid., 24–44.

20. Ibid., 40, 60, 67.

21. On Burton's digressions, see Fox, *The Tangled Chain*, 45–121. She describes them as providing him "with a vantage point inside of, yet removed from, his structure which allows him to see, ponder, and re-evaluate the usefulness of that structure and, indeed, of all 'perfectly' ordered, 'rationally' devised books of knowledge" (113).

22. Hodges, *Renaissance Fictions of Anatomy*, 18.

Chapter Three

1. See Bridget Gellert Lyons, *Voices of Melancholy: studies in literary treatments of melancholy in Renaissance England* (New York: Barnes & Noble, 1971), 2–4.

2. Raymond Klibansky, Erwin Panofsky, and Fritz Saxl have studied this reinterpretation as a background for Dürer's "Melancholia I" in *Saturn and Melancholy* (New York: Basic Books, 1964), esp. 15–41, 254–74).

3. See in particular Michael MacDonald's study of the psychiatric practice of Richard Napier, an astrological physician and clergyman in early seventeenth-century Buckinghamshire, *Mystical Bedlam: madness, anxiety, and healing in seventeenth-century England*.

4. Lawrence Babb, *Sanity in Bedlam: a Study of Robert Burton's* Anatomy of Melancholy (East Lansing: Michigan State University Press, 1959), 18.

5. James Roy King finds "a heavy concentration of dull passages in the medical sections" and suggests this may signal "a fundamental distaste on Burton's part for much of the material to which he had committed himself" (*Studies in Six 17th Century Writers* [Athens, Ohio: Ohio University Press, 1966], 65. Though this may overstate the matter somewhat, it seems true that Burton's imagination is seldom stimulated by the medical and pharmacological sections.

6. David Renaker, "Robert Burton and Ramist Method," *Renaissance Quarterly* 24 (1971):210–20.

7. Simon, *Robert Burton*, 428.

8. In a note Burton gives the Latin of the part he quotes: *Fatendum est cacumine Olympi constitutus supra ventos et procellas, et omnes res humanas.* But whom is he quoting?

9. See especially J. B. Bamborough, "Burton and Cardan," 180–93. Bamborough notes that Burton refers to Cardan over 150 times in the course of the *Anatomy* (more than twice as often as he refers to Aristotle) and suggests that his debt to Cardan is far more significant than to Montaigne, to whom he refers seven times, and Rabelais, whom he probably did not read.

10. David Renaker notes that "Burton felt free to regard each part of his world, for the moment he was treating it, as an absolute, ignoring or forgetting its relation to the others" ("Robert Burton and Ramist Method," 219).

11. Judith Kegan Gardiner, who gives the most balanced summary of Burton's psychology, describes it as primarily "moral and evaluative," a "humanistic psychology that is both comprehensive and reasonably coherent" ("Elizabethan Psychology and Burton's *Anatomy of Melancholy*," *Journal of the History of Ideas* 38 [1977]:373–88). She also notes some suggestive parallels to Spenser's psychology in *The Faerie Queene*.

12. See John L. Lievsay, "Robert Burton's *De Consolatione*," *South Atlantic Quarterly* 55 (1956):329–36, on the tradition behind these essays.

13. Fox, *The Tangled Chain*, 94.

14. Richard G. Barlow details Burton's growing allegiance to the new astronomy and his eventual acceptance, in later editions, of the idea of infinite worlds ("Infinite Worlds: Robert Burton's Cosmic Voyage,"

Journal of the History of Ideas 34 [1973]:291–302). In this he modifies the view of Burton espoused by Robert M. Browne, "Robert Burton and the New Cosmology," *Modern Language Quarterly* 13 (1952):131–48.

15. Fox, *The Tangled Chain*, 128.
16. Ibid., 129.
17. *Utopia*, ed. Edward Surtz and J. H. Hexter, in *Complete Works of St. Thomas More* (New Haven: Yale University Press, 1965), 4:220–21; see also the note on the passage (520), which links the religious universalism of the passage to Ficino, Pico della Miranadola, and Nicholas of Cusa.

Chapter Four

1. Joan Webber in particular emphasizes the oral character of Burton's prose style in her chapter in *The Eloquent "I,"* 80–114.
2. Morris Croll, "The Baroque Style in Prose," *Studies in English Philology*, ed. Kemp Malone and Martin B. Ruud (Minneapolis: University of Minnesota Press, 1929); reprinted in *Style, Rhetoric and Rhythm: Essays by Morris W. Croll*, ed. J. Max Patrick and Robert O. Evans (Princeton: Princeton University Press, 1966), 207–33.
3. Besides the essays by Croll collected in *Style, Rhetoric, and Rhythm*, see also George Williamson, "Senecan Style in the Seventeenth Century," *Philological Quarterly* 15 (1936):321–51, reprinted in *Seventeenth Century Prose*, ed. Stanley E. Fish (New York: Oxford University Press, 1971), 112–46, and chapter 7 of Williamson's *The Senecan Amble: a Study in Prose Form from Bacon to Collier* (Chicago: University of Chicago Press, 1951), 186–230.
4. Lawrence Babb analyzes six passages that Burton revised over the course of six editions and concludes that in each case he fitted new material into the existing arrangement, that "the text is left unchanged or altered just enough to accommodate the interpolations," *Sanity in Bedlam*, 23.
5. Croll, "The Baroque Style, in Prose," in *Style Rhetoric, and Rhythm*, 219–30.
6. See above, p. 18–19.
7. See Simon's discussion, Robert Burton, 469–75.
8. Anthony Hobson, *Great Libraries* (New York: G. P. Putnam's Sons, 1970), 168.
9. Ibid., 170.
10. Leonard Goldstein, "Science and Literary Style in Robert Burton's *'Cento* out of Divers Writers,' " *Journal of the Rutgers University Library* 21 (1958):55–68.

Chapter Five

1. Frederick S. Boas, *University Drama in the Tudor Age* (Oxford: Oxford University Press, 1914; reprint, New York: Benjamin Blom, 1966), 1–25.

2. On the title page of the manuscript, Burton describes the comedy as "Scripta *Anno Domini,* 1606, Alterata, renovata, perfecta *Anno Domini,* 1615." See Paul Jordan-Smith's preface, *Philosophaster,* xii–xiii. All quotations from *Philosophaster* and Burton's other Latin verse are from this edition. Unless otherwise noted, translations from *Philosophaster* are Jordan-Smith's.

3. Simon, *Robert Burton,* 66.

4. Jordan-Smith, *Philosophaster,* xvi.

5. "L'absence d'émotion se dissimule sous le masque de la grandiloquence, et l'aridité de l'inspiration se donne le change par un constant appel à l'imagerie astrologique," *Robert Burton,* 62.

6. The first poem celebrates James's accession, the second his visit to Oxford in 1605; the third mourns the death of Prince Henry; the fourth is an epithalamion for the marriage of Princess Elizabeth to Frederick the elector palatine; the sixth congratulates James on his return from his visit to Scotland in 1617; the seventh mourns the death of Queen Anne; the ninth treats Prince Charles's visit incognito to Spain concerning marriage prospects; the eleventh is on James's death, the twelfth on Charles's marriage to Henrieta Maria; the thirteenth, fifteenth, sixteenth and seventeenth celebrate respectively the births of the future Charles II, of the future James II, and of the Princess Elizabeth (two poems), and the fourteenth concerns Charles's visit to Scotland in 1633.

7. Translations of the commemorative poems are my own; Jordan-Smith translates only *Philosophaster.*

8. Simon faults it for its "laborieux calembours," *Robert Burton,* 63.

9. I am indebted to my colleague John Sullivan, a noted Martial scholar, for pointing Burton's models out to me.

10. The title story of *The Book of Sand,* translated by Norman Thomas di Giovanni (New York: Dutton, 1975). The story is clearly related to Borges' earlier story "The Library of Babel," which takes its epigraph from the *Anatomy* ("By this art you may contemplate the variation of the 23 letters . . ." *Anatomy* 2.2.4).

Selected Bibliography

The bibliography of secondary works concentrates on scholarship of the last thirty-five years, but includes influential or significant earlier works. It omits unpublished dissertations and works in which Burton figures only in a minor way.

PRIMARY SOURCES

1. Early Editions of the *Anatomy*

The Anatomy of Melancholy, what it is. With all the Kindes, Causes, Symptomes, Prognostickes, and several cures of it. Oxford: Henry Cripps, 1621. First edition, in quarto. 880 pages. Contained "Conclusion of the Author to the Reader," omitted in subsequent editions.

————. Oxford: Henry Cripps, 1624. Second edition, in folio. 652 pages.

————. Oxford: Henry Cripps, 1628. Third edition, in folio. 760 pages. Engraved title page.

————. Oxford: Henry Cripps, 1632. Fourth edition, in folio. 882 pages. Engraved title page and "Argument of the Frontispiece."

————. Oxford: Henry Cripps, 1638. Fifth edition, in folio. 840 pages. Engraved title page, etc. This edition was printed partly in Edinburgh, partly in Oxford.

————. Oxford: Henry Cripps, 1651. Sixth, posthumous edition, in folio. 842 pages. Engraved title page, etc. Note by Cripps says that Burton left a copy at his death, "exactly corrected, with several considerable Additions by his own hand."

A seventh edition, in folio, appeared in 1660 and an eighth in 1676. No subsequent edition appeared until a two-volume quarto was published in 1800. After this the *Anatomy* was frequently reprinted throughout the nineteenth century.

2. Modern Editions of the *Anatomy*

The Anatomy of Melancholy. Edited by A. R. Shilleto. London: Bell & Sons, 1893. 3 vols. The standard edition, but containing numerous errors taken from the seventh edition.

————. Edited by Floyd Dell and Paul Jordan-Smith. New York: Farrar & Rinehart, 1927. An all-English edition.

————. Introduction by Holbrook Jackson. Everyman's Library edition. London: J. M. Dent, 1932. Standard popular edition, based on the sixth edition. Contains bracketed translations of the Latin Burton does not translate.

A new scholarly edition of the *Anatomy*, with full textual notes and commentary, is in preparation; it is expected to be published in the late 1980s.

3. Minor Works

Philosophaster, Comoedia; Poemata. Edited by W. E. Buckley for Roxburgh Club, Hertford, 1862. First edition of Burton's Latin comedy and first collected edition of the Latin poems. Only 65 copies printed.

Robert Burton's Philosophaster: with an English translation of the same, together with his other minor writings in prose and verse. Edited by Paul Jordan-Smith. Stanford: Stanford University Press, 1932. Contains all of the minor works.

SECONDARY SOURCES

1. Bibliographical Works

Donovan, Dennis. "Sir Thomas Browne, 1924–1966, Robert Burton, 1924–1966." *Elizabethan Bibliographies Supplement* 10 (1968). Chronological listing of Burton scholarship.

————. "Recent Studies in Burton and Walton." *English Literary Renaissance* 1 (1971):294–303. Brief descriptions of recent work and the state of Burton scholarship.

————; Herman, Magaretha G. Hartley; Imbrie, Ann E. *Sir Thomas Browne and Robert Burton: a Reference Guide.* Boston: G. K. Hall, 1981. Lists chronologically and briefly describes writings by and about Burton from 1621 to 1978. Includes doctoral dissertations and works in which Burton is mentioned.

Gibson, S., and Needham, F. R. D. "Lists of Burton's Library." *Oxford Bibliographical Society, Proceedings and Papers* 1 (1922–26):222–246. Lists Burton's books in Bodleian and Christ Church Libraries. Not entirely complete or accurate. A new list of Burton's library by Nicholas Kiessling is scheduled to be published by the Oxford Bibliographical Society in 1986.

Heventhal, Charles, Jr. "Robert Burton's *Anatomy of Melancholy* in Early America." *Papers of the Bibliographical Society of America* 63 (1969):157–75. An account of copies of the *Anatomy* before the first American edition in 1836.

Jordan-Smith, Paul. *Bibliographia Burtoniana: a Study of Robert Burton's "The Anatomy of Melancholy."* Stanford: Stanford University Press, 1931. An appreciation of Burton with some solid discussion of the sources of the *Anatomy,* a full bibliography of early and modern editions of Burton's works, and a listing of some early criticism.

Kiessling, Nicholas. *"The Anatomy of Melancholy:* Preparations for a New Edition." *Literary Research Newsletter* 4 (1979):181–89. Plans for a new scholarly edition, with textual notes and a full commentary, to be completed by a team of editors with computer assistance; expected in the late 1980s.

Linden, Stanton J. "Robert Burton's Sigil and John Dee." *N.Q.* 227 (1982):415–16. Describes a sigil deriving from John Dee that Burton used to mark several of his books.

2. Biographical Works

Bamborough, J. B. "Robert Burton's Astrological Notebook." *Review of English Studies* n.s. 32 (1981):267–85. Detailed discussion of the volume that Burton used for astrological calculations, including his own nativity.

Burton, William. *The Description of Leicestershire.* London, 1622. Contains reference to Burton estate, family.

Dewey, Nicholas. "Burton's Melancholy: a Paradox Disintered." *Modern Philology* 68:292–93. Argues that the *Melancholia* of Burton's epitaph refers to his book.

Fuller, Thomas. *The Worthies of England.* London, 1662. Earliest biographical account of Burton, very brief.

Hearne, Thomas. *Reliquiae Hearnianae.* Edited by Philip Bliss. Oxford, 1857. Eighteenth-century anecdotes about Burton and his reputation.

Höltgen, Karl Josef. "Robert Burton and the Rectory of Seagrave." *Review of English Studies* 27 (1976):129–36. The date and circumstances of Burton's possession of the living of Seagrave.

Kennett, White. *A Register and Chronicle Ecclesiastical and Civil.* London, 1728. Brief biographical note, including anecdote about Burton's laughing at bargemen.

MS. Marshall 132. Bodleian Library. Manuscript containing Burton family history.

Nochimson, Richard L. "Robert Burton's Authorship of *Alba*: a Lost Letter Recovered." *Review of English Studies* n.s. 2 (1970):325–31. Rediscovery of a portion of a letter Burton wrote to his brother about his part in writing a comedy performed before King James in 1605.

————. "Studies in the Life of Robert Burton." *Yearbook of English Studies* 4 (1974):85–111. Important summary of biographical facts and critique of biographers' errors.

Skeat, T. C. "A Letter of Robert Burton." *British Museum Quarterly* 22 (1960):12–16. Prints a letter of Burton concerning a dispute with one of his parishioners at Seagrave.

Traister, Barbara H. "New Evidence about Burton's Melancholy." *Renaissance Quarterly* 29 (1976):66–70. A twenty-year-old Robert Burton was treated for melancholy by Simon Forman in 1597.

Vicari, E. Patricia. "Saturn Culminating, Mars Ascending: the Fortunate/ Unfortunate Horoscope of Robert Burton." In *Familiar Colloquy: Essays Presented to Arthur Edward Barker,* edited by Patricia Brückmann, 96–112. Ontario: Oberon Press, 1978. Full discussion of Burton's nativity.

Wood, Anthony à. *Athenae Oxonienses.* London, 1813–20. Volume 2 contains an important early biographical memorial of Burton (1691–92).

See also Simon, Jean Robert, below.

3. General

Babb, Lawrence. *Sanity in Bedlam: a Study of Robert Burton's* Anatomy of Melancholy. East Lansing, Mich.: Michigan State University Press, 1959. Critical description containing much solid, useful information.

Bamborough, J. B. *The Little World of Man.* London: Longmans, Green, 1952. Description of Renaissance psychology with frequent reference to Burton.

———. "Burton and Cardan." In *English Renaissance Studies Presented to Dame Helen Gardner in Honour of Her Seventieth Birthday.* Edited by John Carey. Oxford: Oxford University Press, 1980. Significant discussion of Burton's affinity to Cardan in interests, manner, personality, and style.

———. "Burton and Hemingius." *Review of English Studies* n.s. 34 (1983):441–45. Adduces Burton's use of Niels Hemmingsen's *Antidotum adversus pestem desperationis* (1599) in strengthening the conclusion of the *Anatomy.*

Barlow, Richard G. "Infinite Worlds: Robert Burton's Cosmic Voyage." *Journal of the History of Ideas* 34 (1973):291–302. The "Digression of Air" shows Burton's allegiance to the new astronomy and his eventual acceptance, in later editions of the *Anatomy,* of the doctrine of infinite worlds.

Bentley, Christopher. "*The Anatomy of Melancholy* and Richard Whitlock's *Zootomia.*" *Renaissance and Modern Studies* 13 (1969):88–105. Details Whitlock's plagiarism from Burton.

Bright, Timothy. *A Treatise of Melancholie.* London, 1586. Important predecessor of the *Anatomy,* more obviously therapeutic in intention and execution.

Browne, Robert M. "Robert Burton and the New Cosmology." *Modern Language Quarterly* 13 (1952):131–48. In "Digression of Air" Burton shows himself interested in new cosmology and sympathetic to Copernican system, but withholds allegiance because of its implication of infinite worlds. See also Barlow, Richard G.

Brownlee, Alexander. *William Shakespeare and Robert Burton.* Reading: Bodley & Son, 1960. Burton wrote the *Sonnets,* most of *Hamlet* and *Macbeth,* collaborated with Shakespeare on most of the other plays. A curiosity.

Burgess, Anthony. "The Anatomy of Melancholy." *Horizon* 12 (Autumn 1970):48–53. General description for a popular audience.

Bush, Douglas. *English Literature in the Earlier Seventeenth Century, 1600–1660.* Oxford: Oxford University Press, 1945; 2d ed., 1962. Contains a good seven-page introduction to Burton.

Canavan, Thomas L. "Robert Burton, Jonathan Swift, and the Tradition of Anti-Puritan Invective." *Journal of the History of Ideas* 34 (1973):227–42. Places Burton among seventeenth-century writers on religious enthusiasm.

Colie, Rosalie. *Paradoxia Epidemica: the Renaissance Tradition of Paradox.* Princeton: Princeton University Press, 1966. Contains a significant chapter on the *Anatomy* as an example of paradox in its mixture of genres, material, rhetorical strategy, etc.

————. "Some Notes on Burton's Erasmus." *Renaissance Quarterly* 20 (1967):335–41. Examines a copy of Erasmus used by Burton.

Croll, Morris W. *Style, Rhetoric, and Rhythm: Essays by Morris W. Croll.* Edited by J. Max Patrick and Robert O. Evans. Princeton, Princeton University Press, 1966. Classic essays on sixteenth- and seventeenth-century prose style with frequent reference to Burton.

Dewey, Nicholas. " 'Democritus Junior' alias Robert Burton." *Princeton University Library Chronicle* 33 (1970). Argues for the separation of Democritus Junior from the author in understanding Burton's personality.

Donovan, Dennis. "Robert Burton, Anglican Minister." *Renaissance Papers* 1967, 33–39. General description of his opinions, attitudes in *Anatomy.*

Evans, Bergen. *The Psychiatry of Robert Burton.* New York: Columbia University Press, 1944. Attempts to describe Burton's "psychiatry" and compare it with modern theory and practice; dated in conception, misleading in its diagnosis of Burton's personality.

Fish, Stanley E. *Self-Consuming Artifacts: the Experience of Seventeenth-Century Literature.* Berkeley: University of California Press, 1972. Includes a significant chapter arguing that Burton's rhetorical strategy in the Preface is to disorient the reader.

Fox, Ruth A. *The Tangled Chain: the Structure of Disorder in the "Anatomy of Melancholy."* Berkeley: University of California Press, 1976. Most comprehensive account of the structure and rhetorical purposes of the *Anatomy*.

Friederich, Reinhard H. "Training His Melancholy Spaniel: Persona and Structure in Robert Burton's 'Democritus Junior to the Reader.' " *Philological Quarterly* 55 (1976):195–210. Argues that the vagaries of the persona in the Preface comically demonstrate the instability of melancholy/madness.

Gardiner, Judith Kegan. "Elizabethan Psychology and Burton's *Anatomy of Melancholy.*" *Journal of the History of Ideas* 38 (1977):373–88. Perhaps the best description of the psychology of the *Anatomy*, stressing its moral and evaluative character; Burton is not an inconsistent behaviorist but a consistent humanist in his approach to experience and personality.

Gentili, Augusto. "Lettura del frontespizio della 'Anatomy of Melancholy.' " *English Miscellany* 21 (1970):81–98. Argues that Burton's utopianism is a symptom of political and psychological stasis caused by the intellectual dislocations of the century.

Goldstein, Leonard. "Science and Literary Style in Robert Burton's 'Cento out of Diverse Writers.' " *Journal of the Rutgers University Library* 21 (1958):55–68. Argues that the listing characteristic of Burton's style is an unconscious symptom of the quantifying tendencies of Galilean science.

Gottlieb, Hans Jordan. *Robert Burton's Knowledge of English Poetry.* New York: Graduate School of New York University, 1933. Tabulates the references to English poets in the *Anatomy*.

Grace, William J. "Notes on Robert Burton and John Milton." *Studies in Philology* 52 (1955):578–91. Adduces a number of parallels, some tenuous, between the *Anatomy* and Milton's poetry.

Hale, David G. "Robert Burton's Aesop." *N.Q.* 220 (1975):542. Identifies the Latin version Burton used and lists his references to Aesop.

Hodges, Devon L. *Renaissance Fictions of Anatomy.* Amherst: University of Massachusetts Press, 1985. Sophisticated discussion of Renaissance anatomies with significant concluding chapter on Burton.

Hogan, Jerome W. "Robert Burton's Borrowings from John Abernathy's *A Christian and Heavenly Treatise.*" *Neophilologus* 60 (1976), 140–44. Argues for the influence of Abernathy on treatment of despair in *Anatomy* 3.4.2–6. See also Stackniewski, John.

Höltgen, Karl Josef. "Robert Burton and the *Islandiae Descriptio* of Dithmar 'Bleskenius.' " *English Studies* 62 (1981):423–28. Identifies Burton's "Bleskenius" as Ditmar Blefken, who wrote a fanciful account of Iceland.

Idol, John L., Jr. "Burton's Illustrative Use of Emblems." *Renaissance Papers* (1979), 19–28. Reproduces twenty-five emblems referred to in the text of the *Anatomy*.

King, James Roy. *Studies in Six 17th Century Writers*. Athens, Ohio: Ohio University Press, 1966. Includes a significant chapter on Burton arguing that the *Anatomy* was composed of disparate essays joined to medical materials; sees underlying disunity in book.

Kinsman, Robert S. "Folly, Melancholy, and Madness: a Study in Shifting Styles of Medical Analysis and Treatment, 1450–1675." In *The Darker Vision of the Renaissance*. Edited by Robert S. Kinsman. Berkeley: University of California Press, 1974. A survey in which Burton figures prominently.

Klibansky, Raymond; Panofsky, Erwin; Saxl, Fritz. *Saturn and Melancholy: Studies in the History of Natural Philosophy, Religion and Art*. New York: Basic Books, 1964. Intellectual history of melancholy from the ancient world down to the Renaissance as background to Dürer's "Melancholia I."

Korkowski, Bud. "Genre and Satiric Strategy in Burton's *Anatomy of Melancholy*." *Genre* 8 (1979):74–87. Argues that the genre of the entire *Anatomy* is Menippean satire.

Laurens, André du [Laurentinus, Andreas]. *A Discourse of the Preservation of the Sight; of Melancholike diseases; of Rheumes, and Old Age*. London, 1599. English translation of French work on melancholy (1594), one of Burton's important sources on melancholy.

Lievsay, John L. "Robert Burton's *De Consolatione*." *South Atlantic Quarterly* 55 (1956):329–36. Considers *Anatomy* 2.3 as part of the tradition of consolatory literature.

Lyons, Bridget Gellert. *Voices of Melancholy: Studies in Literary Treatments of Melancholy in Renaissance England*. New York: Barnes & Noble, 1971. Discussion of the sixteenth-century background of melancholy with a significant chapter on the *Anatomy* as a literary portrayal of its subject.

MacDonald, Michael. *Mystical Bedlam: Madness, Anxiety, and Healing in Seventeenth-century England*. Cambridge: Cambridge University Press, 1981. Considers the social implications of the career of Richard Napier, a contemporary of Burton who treated hundreds of cases of mental illness.

Mueller, William R. "Robert Burton's Frontispiece." *PMLA* 64 (1949):1074–88. Glosses the engravings by reference mainly to the text of the *Anatomy*.

———. *The Anatomy of Robert Burton's England*. University of California Publications in English Studies: 2. Berkeley: University of California Press, 1952. Argues that the *Anatomy* is a serious commentary on the political, economic, social, and religious problems of seventeenth-century England.

————. "Robert Burton's 'Satyrical Preface.' " *Modern Language Quarterly* 15 (1954):28–35. A general description.

Nochimson, Richard. "Burton's *Anatomy*: the Author's Purposes and the Reader's Response." *Forum for Modern Language Studies* 13 (1977):265–84. Significant discussion of the ways Burton uses his persona to mask insecurities and manipulate the reader's response.

Osler, Sir William. "Burton's *Anatomy of Melancholy*." *Yale Review* 3 (1914):251–71. An influential description.

————. "Robert Burton: the Man, his Book, his Library." *Oxford Bibliographical Society,* Proceedings and Papers 1 (1922–26):162–90. Expanded version of *Yale Review* essay, with material on Burton's library.

Patrick, J. Max. "Robert Burton's Utopianism." *Philological Quarterly* 27 (1948):345–58. Study of the sources and development of utopian section of Preface to *Anatomy*.

Ravignani, Donatella. "Ford e Burton: riesame di un rapporto." *English Miscellany* 17 (1966):211–47. Ford begins with a heavy reliance on Burton but grows more independent in the psychology of his later plays.

Renaker, David. "Robert Burton and Ramist Method." *Renaissance Quarterly* 24 (1971):210–20. Burton used Ramist logic in his synoptic charts—then virtually ignored it in his text.

————. "Robert Burton's Tricks of Memory." *PMLA* 87 (1972):391–96. Burton's memory causes unconscious exaggerations and transformations of his material in the *Anatomy*.

————. "Fontenelle and Burton: a Shared Simile and a Missing Link." *N.Q.* 222 (1977):207–8. The same simile for the Milky Way in each, but no explanation available to explain the coincidence.

————. "Robert Burton's Palinodes." *Studies in Philology* 76 (1979):162–81. Argues that Burton outlines an Arminian position in his Cure of Despair (*Anatomy* 3.2.4.6), then protects himself with an extreme Calvinist palinode.

————. "Robert Burton versus Owen Felltham on Documentation." *N.Q.* 227 (1982):416–17. Burton may have Felltham in mind in his polemical additions to his prefatory defense of his method of citing authors.

Simon, Jean Robert. *Robert Burton (1577–1640) et "L'Anatomie de la Mélancholie."* Paris: Didier, 1964. Most comprehensive study of Burton's life, the *Anatomy,* and minor works.

Stackniewski, John. "Robert Burton's Use of John Abernathy's *A Christian and Heavenly Treatise.*" *Neophilologus* 62 (1978):634–36. Critiques

Jerome W. Hogan, argues Burton was cavalier in his use of Abernathy.

Starobinski, Jean. "La Mélancholie de L'Anatomiste." *Tel Quel* 10 (1962):21–29. A suggestive discussion, centered on Burton, of the marginality of the melancholy satirist.

Ward, Aileen. "Keats and Burton: a Reappraisal." *Philological Quarterly* 40 (1961):535–52. Keats came to the *Anatomy* later than has been thought and was influenced less in his poetry than in his emotional life.

Webber, Joan. *The Eloquent "I": Style and Self in Seventeenth-Century Prose.* Madison: University of Wisconsin Press, 1968. Contains an important discussion of Burton's creation of a voice and personality in the *Anatomy*.

Williamson, George. "Senecan Style in the Seventeenth Century." *Philological Quarterly* 15 (1936):321–51. Description of the dominant fashion of prose style in the early century.

―――. *The Senecan Amble: a Study in Prose Form from Bacon to Collier.* Chicago: University of Chicago Press, 1951. Longer study with some reference to Burton's "loose" Senecan style.

Index

Voice, spoken: imitated in Burton's prose:
75, 78, 80, 88–89, 90–91. *See also* Colloquial language, Style, Syntax

Walesby, Lincolnshire, 10, 21
Webber, Joan, 36, 47, 115n1

Wilkins, John, 17, 96
Williamson, George, 115n3
Wolsey, Thomas, 15
Wood, Anthony à, 9, 18, 21, 24, 29, 30,
31, 35, 43, 80